Life in the Treetops

Adventures of a Woman in Field Biology

MARGARET D. LOWMAN

Yale University Press / New Haven & London

Frontispiece: Above a forest in Cameroon, Margaret Lowman reclines on a treetop lab of netting attached to a hot-air balloon. Photo by H. Bruce Rinker.

Published with assistance from the Mary Cady Tew Memorial Fund.

Designed by Nancy Ovedovitz and set in Galos type by The Composing Room of Michigan, Inc. Printed in the United States of America.

Library of Congress Cataloging-in-Publication Data
Lowman, Margaret D.
Life in the treetops : adventures of a woman in field biology / Margaret D. Lowman ; foreword by Robert Ballard.
p.   cm.
Includes bibliographical references and index.
ISBN 0-300-07818-8 (cloth : alk. paper)
1. Lowman, Margaret D.   2. Ecologists—Australia—Biography.   3. Women ecologists—Australia—Biography.
4. Rain forest ecology.   5. Forest canopy ecology.
I. Title.
QH31.L79A3   1999
577.34'092—dc21
[B]   98-48691

A catalogue record for this book is available from the British Library.

The paper in this book meets the guidelines for permanence and durability of the Committee on Production Guidelines for Book Longevity of the Council of Library Resources.

10 9 8 7 6 5 4

For Eddie and James, my children and field assistants, who help me retain my sense of wonder for nature. And for Michael, who taught me how to bridge the links between science and spirit.

Contents

Foreword

Our planet Earth is unique among its smaller, stony sister planets Venus, Mars, and Mercury. For Earth, unlike the others, supports a vast diversity of life.

For the past thirty years I have spent my professional career exploring our planet, discovering its many wonders. Those explorations have taken me to its vast deserts, to the top of its snow-covered peaks, to its shrouded forests, and across its great plains. But because more than two-thirds of our planet is covered with water, I have spent most of my time exploring its hidden landscape beneath the sea. I have used deep-diving submersibles to investigate undersea volcanoes that run along the axis of immense submerged mountain ranges — underwater masses that cover almost a quarter of the planet's surface. Within those mountains I have discovered exotic marine life living in total darkness, life that is not dependent on the energy of the sun, but life that has learned how to harvest Earth's internal energy through a process known as chemosynthesis.

Although I find the deep sea a fascinating place to explore, a place where I am able to learn a great deal about our planet,

I have come to realize one important truth. It is a truth the astronauts learned when they traveled to the far side of the moon: no matter how large the Universe may be, Earth is our spaceship in life. Earth is where mankind came into the world and where the children of future generations will live.

Within Earth itself, I have learned that it is the land surface of the planet that will always be our home. We may venture forth to explore the majority of our planet that lies beneath the waves, but we will always come back to the surface to breathe its fresh air, bask in the warmth of the sun, and eat from its lush green table.

In 1994 I had a unique opportunity to leave my tiny submarine for a few months and live in the canopy of a tropical rain forest in the small Central American country of Belize. My personal guide for this wonderful experience was Margaret Lowman, a canopy biologist who has dedicated her life to better understanding the role that tropical rain forests play in the planet's interconnected ecosystem.

Our reason for working together, one hundred feet above the rainforest floor, was the Jason Project, an annual electronic field trip that uses the latest in telecommunications technology so that more than five hundred thousand students and twelve thousand teachers worldwide can participate in "live" exploration. For two weeks I watched Meg share her knowledge and enthusiasm with participating students and teachers, several of whom actually joined us on our canopy platform. For hours on end Meg showed them the secrets of life, from tiny leaf-eating organisms to the tallest of trees within the rain forest. Through her words students learned to comprehend more fully their role as shepherds of the planet, entrusted with the awesome responsibility of not only preserving the lungs of the Earth, but in so doing also preserving the human race.

As we left the beautiful forest of Belize and lowered ourselves one last time from the tiny canopy platform that had become our home,

I realized I had met a superb scientist, an excellent role model for young women, a kind human, and a new friend.

Robert D. Ballard
Director, Center for Marine Exploration
Mystic, Connecticut

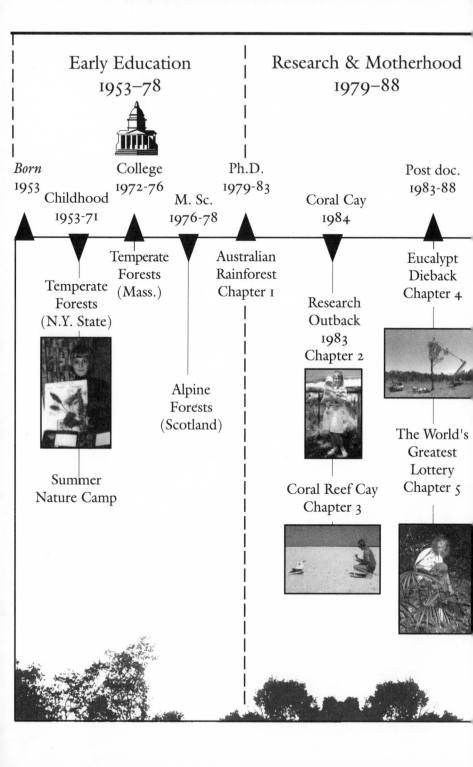

Early Education
1953–78

Research & Motherhood
1979–88

Born
1953

Childhood
1953-71

College
1972-76

M. Sc.
1976-78

Ph.D.
1979-83

Coral Cay
1984

Post doc.
1983-88

Temperate
Forests
(N.Y. State)

Temperate
Forests
(Mass.)

Australian
Rainforest
Chapter 1

Research
Outback
1983
Chapter 2

Eucalypt
Dieback
Chapter 4

Alpine
Forests
(Scotland)

Summer
Nature Camp

Coral Reef Cay
Chapter 3

The World's
Greatest
Lottery
Chapter 5

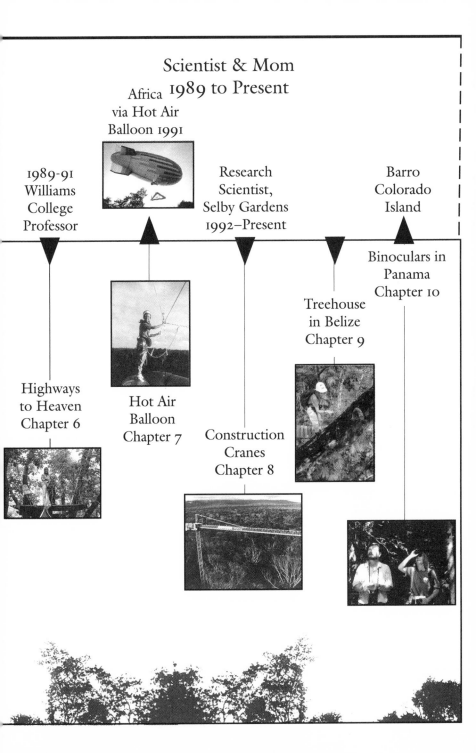

Scientist & Mom
1989 to Present

Africa via Hot Air Balloon 1991

1989-91 Williams College Professor

Research Scientist, Selby Gardens 1992–Present

Barro Colorado Island

Binoculars in Panama Chapter 10

Treehouse in Belize Chapter 9

Highways to Heaven Chapter 6

Hot Air Balloon Chapter 7

Construction Cranes Chapter 8

Preface

My career is not conventional; I climb trees. Nor does my job follow a normal nine-to-five schedule. My children have been extraordinary in their patience and flexibility, managing to find security despite their mother's frenzied pace; but they have been secure in their home, which abounds with unconditional love. My forays into the jungle were frequent and usually turned our household upside down — before I departed, by last-minute packing of malaria tablets and mosquito netting, or upon my return, by struggles with jetlag and parasites that had invaded my system. But during field trips my parents and a host of loyal, supportive friends saw to it that continuity and stability were maintained in my household. I feel lucky that I was never knocked unconscious by a falling coconut, was never bitten by an Australian brown snake, and never fell out of a tall tree (just small ones!). Still, there have been other pitfalls in the course of my journey as both a scientist and a parent. I have learned that the physical hazards of field biology are not nearly as challenging as the emotional issues. I was fortunate to find that success as a scientist does not preclude the important family values of love and sharing. It is simply a balancing act that, nurtured by passion and a love of life, creates a sense of wonder in our everyday life. And I hope that my contributions as a scientist working on rain-forest conservation will leave the world a slightly better place for my children and their children to live.

I am grateful to the many colleagues whose ideas and creativity over the years have continually inspired me: Heidi Appel, Peter Ashton, John Atwood, Mark Bierner, Bart Bouricius, Hugh Caffey, Joe Connell, Nate Erwin, Robin Foster, Laurel Fox, Francis Hallé, Bruce and Anna Marie Hatcher, Hal Heatwole, Bruce Holst, Harry Luther, Mark Moffett, Patrice Morrow, Nalini Nadkarni, Mike Pender, Bruce Rinker, Brian Rosborough, Jack Schultz, Lee and John Trott, Tony Underwood, Joanna Wurtele, Joe Wright, and others. Ellen Baskerville, Beryl Black, Jessa Fisher, John Trott, and the members of my tutorial in Women and Nature Writing at Williams College kindly volunteered to read some of the chapters. And Barbara Harrison skillfully prepared many of the figures for the book.

It has been an inspiration to work with Jean Thomson Black, my editor at Yale University Press; and Vivian Wheeler miraculously edited the manuscript into its current form. Thank you both for your dedication.

Perhaps most of all, I am indebted to my children, Eddie and James, for keeping me curious about the natural world, and to my parents, who patiently tended my household during many weeks of tree-climbing research. Without them I could not have been both a scientist and a parent.

And Michael Brown, thank you for getting your boots muddy with me!

Life in the Treetops

Introduction

> Botany needs help from the tropics. Its big plants will engender big thinking.
> —E. H. J. Corner, Cambridge University, 1939

As a child, I collected and classified every conceivable sort of organism: butterflies, birds, insects, shells, nests, even twigs. My parents were not scientists, but they were sympathetic enough to stop the car whenever I saw a collectible bit of roadside nature. Much to my mother's horror, mice lived in my bedroom cupboards. They were obviously delighted with all the natural fibers available in my collections for their nests during the cold winters of upstate New York. My life was blessed with the treasures of nature, and my collections formed the basis of a scientific curiosity. As a fifth grader, I won second prize in the New York state science fair. Wedged shyly in the science fair hall among predominantly boys with electronic experiments and chemistry displays, I felt very proud of my wildflower collection and the distinction it brought to my otherwise modest life.

During my formative teenage years, I was fortunate enough to attend a summer camp devoted to the study of nature; there I met other young people who shared my interest in field biology and remain lifelong colleagues in environmental vocations. The camp directors, John and Lee Trott, produced a legacy of biologists and science educators. Any camp director who can read Aldo Leopold aloud on a hilltop at sunset to thirty gawky teenagers with their hormones raging, and inspire absolute silence and attention, is a charismatic and gifted teacher. John Trott was precisely that.

Although before age twenty I had never traveled beyond America, my curiosity about the natural world led me to Scotland for a master's degree in ecology. My advisor, Peter Ashton, with his infectious enthusiasm for tropical plants, influenced me to direct my doctoral studies to tropical rain forests. Peter advocated living and working in a country that harbored tropical ecosystems, so I chose Australia for my graduate studies. It was there that I completed a Ph.D. on herbivory in rain-forest canopies. I had the honor of collaborating with Joseph Connell, who became my third mentor and inspired me with his ability to design rigorous ecological field experiments. It was also there that I married, became a parent, and confronted the dilemmas of motherhood versus homemaker versus career. I spent almost a decade during the 1980s as an Australian wife and mother.

These chapters are the end result of many hours in my Australian kitchen contemplating why I was washing dishes and picking up Lego pieces while my American counterparts were presenting papers at conferences, utilizing day care, relying on fast foods when they stayed late in the lab, and otherwise managing more successfully to mesh a professional life and family. I loved being a mother and wife, but my soul retained its passion for science.

In 1989 I became uneasy. My full-time commitment to house-wifery — traditional in rural Australia — was intellectually unsatisfying. It was becoming difficult to integrate what I valued in life with the fulltime commitments of Australian rural life. I came to the uncomfortable realization that my principles had been compromised. It was more important that I serve my husband morning tea and a hot lunch than it was to work on a scientific manuscript; I could not afford to buy my children many books because they were so expensive; my father-in-law cut down the hundred-year-old elms in our garden without my consent (their shade had been the mainstay of my existence as a housewife); the wool market collapsed because of the world political situation; my son Eddie claimed one day that women were not capable of becoming doctors; and my husband advised me to stop driving the family car to the university library because my research was not a priority. After having trained more than half my life to be a scientist, the goal was eluding my grasp. I recognized that it was difficult for my Australian family to tolerate a daughter-in-law who loved science and asked intellectual questions in a traditional male arena. So I made the difficult choice to leave the beautiful open spaces of the outback and the Australian forests I had come to love, and to seek intellectual freedom back in the United States. There were many emotional upheavals associated with this difficult decision — to leave my husband, to change continents, to return to the workforce, to resume a career that requires extensive travel and time in remote situations, and to take on the urgent challenges of conservation issues. In this book I share a few of my adventures as a field biologist seeking to balance a career and a family.

Although it is more conventional to write a personal account at the end of one's life, I believe that my perspectives on women in science are more vivid confronted at the height of my career, when my emotions can speak between the lines. The integration of love and family and vocation remains an enormous challenge to both men and women, and cannot be relegated to quiet contemplation during one's sunset years.

Forest canopies have been characterized as one of the last biotic frontiers on Earth. Although they have engendered a great deal of romantic attention, tree crowns have escaped scientific study over the last hundred years because of the logistical challenges of access. During the last decade methods for canopy access — ranging from ropes to platforms to cranes to balloons — have greatly improved. The stage is set to study the mysteries of forest canopies: their inhabitants, their flowers and fruits, their growth and mortality, their medicines and foods, and their intricate patterns of diversity in a three-dimensional, aboveground realm.

Each chapter in this volume features one canopy-access technique, and one or more scientific hypotheses that I was addressing in my research. The chapters are organized in chronological fashion, tracing my canopy career from early days with ropes in Australia (1979), to using a cherry picker to access eucalypt canopies while I was pregnant (1984), to researching via hot-air balloon in Africa (1991), to building treetop walkways in the temperate forests of Massachusetts (1992) and the tropical rain forests of Belize (1994). From these experiences I hope the reader will gain a perspective on how both the methods and sampling designs, as well as the quality of results, have improved over time. Scientists have advanced from solo research efforts to large-scale collaborations in which teams of scientists work together on complex environmental problems. Field experiments are more ambitious, reflecting the cooperative nature of new projects. These are exciting times for field biology!

Over the past fifteen years I have been involved in many pioneering aspects of canopy research on several continents. I have "test-driven" most of the major access techniques (many still in their infancy) and authored more than fifty scientific, peer-reviewed publications. Armed with my arsenal of experience, I wanted to write about the excitement of forest canopies for nonscientific audiences, to share my adventures in the jungle, and especially to present a woman's perspective on a traditionally male career. I hope this volume will offer readers a sense of how a field biologist works and also serve as a stimulus for young people to contemplate a career in science.

In 1982 Andrew Mitchell published a book, *The Enchanted Canopy*, that integrated the canopy experiences of a handful of biologists (myself included) who dared to climb tall trees. In 1986 Donald Perry followed up with a personal volume, *Life above the Forest Floor*, featuring his pioneering exploits with single ropes in neotropical canopies. Almost ten years later Mark Moffett expanded on Mitchell's volume with another illustrated book, *The High Frontier*, that encapsulated the burgeoning number of canopy-access techniques and the researchers involved. In the hope of contributing to this literature on canopy research, but not repeating what already exists, I have added to Perry's first-hand narratives of canopy research fifteen years ago, but provided my own accounts of the current challenges of canopy research from a woman's point of view. For example, how does it feel to dangle precariously from a rope for hours on end, looking in vain for a specific beetle that feeds on sassafras leaves? What is it like to live in an African jungle camp with forty-nine other scientists, all male? Is it possible to balance child rearing with the commitments of tropical field botany?

Life in the Treetops may be viewed from a variety of perspectives: in a biology class, as research on forest canopies; in a humanities class, as an account that features women and science; or in environmental science, as a global case study. In each section of the book I suggest possible avenues for future research. Perhaps of greatest importance, the book is intended for readers who are curious about the world around them, particularly the complex political-sociological-economic-biological issues of forests.

Professional and personal issues invariably overlap. On the professional side, tropical biology was developing rapidly from an infant science over the past twenty years. In the tropics, canopy studies went from a pioneer stage in which everyone worked on methods to access the treetops, to a more mature phase in which field studies can be conducted.

On the personal side, it was perhaps unrealistic of me to contemplate balancing a career plus a family in rural Australia, where such an aspiration was considered bizarre. Juggling the personal and professional aspects of life was a formidable challenge for me, simply because the notion of a professional woman was not socially acceptable. In outback Australia in the 1970s and 1980s, a woman's primary duty was to manage the household. Because of my passion for botany, I never quite fit in. I tried to apply science to my household organization: Could I design a field experiment in my head while washing the dishes? Could I mesh naptime with writing a scientific article? Could I couple pushing the baby carriage with checking a new leaf flush in my experimental plot? This frenzied schedule resulted in a distinct partitioning of my brain. I believe that many women who juggle children and a career learn to compartmentalize their activities. Today the roles of mommy-at-home and daddy-at-work are less distinct, and couples work out myriad variations on this traditional role-playing. For the first time in history, young women in science have the benefit of the advice of an older generation of women scientists. When I was a student, all of my mentors were men — who could hardly advise me about balancing pregnancy with fieldwork or offer helpful hints about living in the jungle with male colleagues.

Different questions drove me as a scientist, and were responsible for my passion to study trees. Why are tropical forests so diverse, as compared to their temperate counterparts? How do insects find their food plants? Do insects affect forest health and lead to long-term global changes? The challenges of sampling in tall trees, in complex forests, in remote jungles, and often in the absence of any creature comforts created considerable adventure in my life. The personal issues of marriage, parenting, and women's roles as perceived by different cultures created additional barriers. But these issues also forced me to develop strong convictions as I made my choices along the pathway through adulthood.

1 The Rain-Forest Canopies of Australia

Yet another continent of life remains to be discovered, not upon the earth, but one to two hundred feet above it, extending over thousands of square miles . . . there awaits a rich harvest for the naturalist who overcomes the obstacles — gravitation, ants, thorns, rotten trunks — and mounts to the summits of the jungle trees.
— William Beebe, G. Inness Hartley, and Paul G. Howes, *Tropical Wild Life in British Guiana,* 1917

My love affair with the rain forest did not begin with the canopy. When I first arrived in Australia in 1978 and began my graduate studies in 1979, I never gave a single thought to the notion of climbing trees, let alone studying what lives up there. I was passionately interested in rain forests, but (like most of my colleagues who aspired to understand the tropics) my horizons were limited by the age-old tradition of making observations at ground level and occasionally using binoculars.

Like most students, I yearned to study the dynamic, cuddly inhabitants of the forest—the monkeys (koalas, in the case of Australia), birds, or even butterflies. Instead, I selected a more benign, yet essential, element—the plants. Several popular accounts have told of women scientists who work with apes or other animals, but I thought that plants deserved a chance, too. I considered them to be as adventurous and passionate as their faunal counterparts. Marvelous twisting vines travel hundreds of meters atop the canopy; aggressive strangler figs wrap around host trees and suffocate them; bromeliad tanks provide watery homes for frogs and salamanders and insects; tiny thrips fly long distances fraught with danger to locate specific flowers for pollination. In short, the lives of plants are full of a mystery that rivals that of any mammal. Perhaps best of all, the tropical rain forest boasts a level of activity and complexity unrivaled anywhere on the planet, and it has become a lifelong challenge to me and others seduced by its botanical mysteries.

During the 1970s, tropical rain forests were still considered a biological black box (in other words, a big dark region full of unknown phenomena). How many species existed in these complex forests? What mechanisms led to the coexistence of so many creatures in one place? Could we understand the intricate relationships between animals and plants in the rain forest before all were destroyed? As a botany student, I found the tropics compelling. Armed with a tolerance for mud, leeches, and damp notebooks, I wanted to confront the enigmas of this poorly understood ecosystem.

My childhood and undergraduate education took place in the more familiar forests of upstate New York, where the annual shedding of leaves and the reliable spring renewal of foliage brought great comfort. A product of the temperate zone throughout my childhood, I suffered the malady typical of many field biologists: a temperate bias. I perceived nature based on what I observed in temperate ecosystems, and this limitation made it difficult to fathom the complexities of tropical forests. Patterns such as evergreen leaves, continuous flowering, winter migrant-bird populations, and leaf fall in December were much harder for me to accept than the convenient summer-winter contrasts of northern temperate maple forests. My graduate studies took me to an unknown forest type, halfway around the world and in a different hemisphere. From this adventure I hoped to gain a clearer picture of some of the complexities of the particular black box called the tropical rain forest.

I had completed a master's degree in ecology in 1978 at University of Aberdeen in Scotland, writing a thesis about the seasonality of highland birch trees. I had huddled under my electric blanket in a student house with no heat or hot water, and often lived on "roadkill" (rabbit stew collected on the roadside after class) to offset my subsistence budget. Like many graduate students, I endured less than acceptable physical conditions in order to gain the opportunity to study new ideas and, in this case, an entirely new continent of plants and animals. Appreciative of the opportunity to thaw out after the chill of the Scottish highlands, and at the same time eager to study tropical forests, I accepted a scholarship from the botany department at the University of Sydney. I was so naive, however, that I failed to realize that Sydney was more than a thousand kilometers from the tropics. Off I went in October 1978 to the land down under, to pursue my botanical dreams.

I had selected Australia as my first site for rain-forest research for several reasons. It was English speaking. Its forests remained some of the least studied in the world. It boasted superb ecological gradients from cool rain forests on the mountaintops to lowland rain forests in the humid valleys, and inland to dry forest on the west-facing slopes. In addition, what aspiring biologist is not fascinated by an island continent abounding with such unique creatures as koalas, wallabies, and cassowaries, to name but a few. I chose to work in the "lucky country," as Australians affectionately call their part of the world — perhaps lucky for a white male, but not for an American woman scientist in the 1970s. I never thought about the cultural challenges: an outback attitude that rigidly segregated gender roles, and a pioneering philosophy that was admirable yet emulated the American West of the last century where issues such as conservation were sometimes overlooked.

In an evolutionary sense, Australia is intriguing because it represents the interface of two groups of plants, the tropical flora from Indonesia and a temperate floral element originating in Antarctica and New Zealand. This overlap provides a relatively high diversity within one continent, and associations of plants found nowhere else on the globe. Australia is also one of the few developed, English-speaking nations to have tropical rain forests. One might assume that it could serve as a model for other countries in terms of excellence in tropical rain-forest management and conservation. In reality, like many other countries, Australia has made mistakes in its attempts to manage natural resources. As recently as the late 1970s, only a handful of individuals had attempted to study its tropical rain forests, and virtually none had ventured into the canopy.

The first challenge of my research career in Australia was to locate and recognize a rain forest, not necessarily a simple task for a student afflicted with temperate bias! My graduate supervisor, Peter Myerscough, a gentleman botanist of English origin and a wonderful teacher, suggested that I simply drive north from Sydney until the foliage became lush green. Such instructions, albeit simple, seemed daunting in a country of 7,682,300 square kilometers (almost as large as the United States at 9,809,390 square kilometers). But his advice was useful, since 95 percent of forests in Australia were a bluish-gray color, from the genus *Eucalyptus* that constituted the dry, or sclerophyll, forest.

The remaining 5 percent of the forests on this island continent were rain forests with a luxuriant green canopy. Rain forest was distributed in a narrow band along the coastal escarpment of eastern Australia. The mountain ranges spanning the northeast coastline created a rain shadow with moisture adequate to support rain-forest vegetation. By definition, rain forests receive over 2,000 millimeters of rainfall annually. In evolutionary history, tropical rain forest was once spread over much of the continent of Australia. This land mass (part of Oceania) was then called Gondwanaland, and its forests were continuous with Indonesia. Tree species of a tropical nature were defined as the Indo-Malaysian element of Australian vegetation; a second component of flora existed in southeastern Australia, called cool temperate or Antarctic (the term *Antarctic* refers to its proximity to the continent of Antarctica). It was composed of flora shared among Chile, New Zealand, and southeastern Australia. These two contrasting vegetation types, the Indo-Malaysian and Antarctic elements, overlapped on one continent to make up the Australian rain-forest flora. Despite their small land area, rain-forest patches in Australia represent a relatively high proportion of the country's floral diversity as compared to their dry-forest counterparts.

During the Jurassic period, drier conditions in Australia resulted in expansion of the dry sclerophyll forest distribution and subsequent reduction of the rain forests. Many of those naturally occurring rain-forest patches have since been reduced or even removed entirely, owing to logging and clearing for agriculture. In the mid-1800s, "timber-getters" cleared and settled many sections of eastern Australia in their search for red cedar (*Toona ciliata,* family Meliaceae), a highly desirable furniture wood. The isolated patches (many along steep gullies) of rain forest that remain today in Australia are a consequence of evolution, as well as of human exploitation.

I did not set out to be a canopy biologist. As my research developed, a natural progression of ideas simply led me into the treetops. My initial forays into the bush were frustrating, because I had few colleagues. No other students and no faculty at the University of Sydney were involved in rain-forest research, so my information came either from books or from fortuitous interactions with visiting scientists. When first contemplating the immensity of designing a doctoral project, I was determined to study butterflies in the rain-forest canopy. I envisioned myself sitting in a swing up in the foliage, counting colorful species of Lepidoptera and having a wonderful time. My supervisor was more realistic and reminded me that a dissertation required extensive data collection. He worried that I might go to the rain forest and find no butterflies, because of their mobility and cryptic behavior. I reluctantly switched to something less mobile: trees. I decided to study the growth patterns of rain-forest leaves, which was an expansion of my master's work in Scotland on phenology (seasonality) and photosynthesis of birch trees — although tree canopies in the highlands of Scotland had been only 15 feet high!

Little information about rain-forest leaves existed in the literature, despite the fact that foliage was the driving force of a forest ecosystem. Prior to the 1970s, the majority of ecological work in rain forests had been descriptive rather than experimental. What were the growth patterns or seasonal dynamics of leaves? They included birth, survival, longevity, death, and decay. My hope was that it would be possible to employ valid experimental design in my research if I dealt with leaves as units of replication rather than entire trees which were too large and cumbersome to replicate with ease.

As is typical of a dedicated graduate student who was passionate about her research, I literally threw myself into fieldwork, living and breathing data and ideas on rain-forest canopies. My aim was to understand the leaf-growth dynamics of the most common tree species in the rain forests in the tropics and subtropics of Eastern Australia, and to measure the impact of herbivores on the survival of leaves. My questions included: What was the lifespan of a leaf in a tropical tree canopy? What factors triggered leaf flush events? What influences caused leaves to die in this warm environment, where winter cold obviously did not trigger abscission?

To answer these questions, I marked thousands of leaves in the canopy, giving careful attention to sampling design with respect to factors such as space (differences between species, sites, heights in the trees, individual trees, among branches) and time (differences in leaf growth with respect to seasons and years). I selected five tree species for comparisons of leaf growth dynamics, mainly because I could not possibly study all of the thousands that constituted the tropical forest canopy. All five species were ecologically important and possessed traits reputed to protect them from insect damage (for example, nasty stinging hairs, extreme toughness, rarity, or toxicity). Over time I documented the battles of my marked leaves against herbivores, which were a major influence on longevity. Little did I know that some of my leaves would have lifespans of over twelve years, making the duration of my fieldwork much longer than anticipated.

Such surprises were indicative of that temperate bias formulated during my youth in upstate New York, where leaves lived only six to eight months.

To test various hypotheses about leaf growth dynamics in rain forests, I could have selected leaves at ground level for my measurements. But it is arguable that my results would have been biased to shady conditions, and atypical of most foliage that grew high above the forest floor in a sunny environment. Gazing upward from ground level, I saw another compelling reason to investigate the canopy rather than limit my research to the forest floor: most of the biodiversity was concentrated in the treetops. Herbivores may be important to the growth dynamics of leaves. Evidence collected in the late 1970s by Terry Erwin of the Smithsonian Institution suggested that the majority of insects on Earth inhabited the forest canopy. My curiosity about the canopy was reinforced by this potential plethora of insect–plant interactions.

I did not intend to climb trees as a career. In fact, I tried desperately to think of alternatives to climbing — such as training a monkey, utilizing large telephoto cameras on pulleys, or working along cliff edges where rain-forest treetops were at eye level before cascading into valleys below. None of these methods seemed feasible for accurate data collection, so I finally decided to become an arbornaut!

I shall never forget my first climb. The date was March 4, 1979 (my mother's birthday), and the tree was a coachwood (*Ceratopetalum apetalum,* family Cunoniaceae). This species grew to 30 meters in Royal National Park just south of Sydney. By good fortune, excellent patches of coastal warm-temperate rain forest remained there, despite urban sprawl. I intended to use this local site for photosynthesis measurements and other studies that might benefit from the close proximity of the University of Sydney. Coachwood, one of my five study species, was an economically important timber species, with tough waxy leaves that looked as though they would be difficult for insects to chew.

I was fortunate enough to be "adopted" by a local spelunking club, whose members taught me about hardware and ropes for climbing even though their techniques had been developed for underground caves. They must have found my ignorance and naiveté quite amusing. Because mountaineering shops and catalogs for outdoor products were not yet available in Australia, I sewed my first harness by hand from seat-belt webbing, following the advice of my teachers, Julia James and Al Warrild. After a practice session in a tree outside the botany department at the University of Sydney, we mounted an aerial expedition into a coachwood, where I learned to rig a tree with a slingshot and rappel. As with most beginners, my first climb was fraught with flailing, upside-down maneuvers as I struggled to center my body weight in a position conducive to dangling from a rope. The sensation was superb — despite all my sore muscles the next day!

From then on, I never looked back . . . or down! After further instruction I thought myself capable of reaching the leaves of any structurally sound tree in the Australian rain forest. Armed with such paraphernalia as 70 meters of Bluewater II static climbing rope, my homemade harness, two Jumars, a whales-tail, a homemade slingshot, a large supply of sinkers and fishline, and field notebooks, I was ready to study life in the treetops.

During my years of canopy research in Australia, I drove hundreds of thousands of kilometers to conduct monthly monitoring of leaves in the canopies of many trees in temperate, subtropical, and tropical rain forests. I developed a permanent list of useful field equipment (see Appendix). These excursions also afforded me the opportunity to see life in the outback, and to embrace the culture of this island continent. I encountered many people whose kindness enriched my field experiences and forever touched my heart: the ranger who of-

Single-rope technique used to complete my Ph.D. research on leaf growth and insect damage in Australian rain-forest canopies. The technique is relatively inexpensive and simple, which makes it popular among graduate students. It requires ropes, technical hardware, and a good aim with a slingshot to propel the line over the support branch. Photograph by Robert Prochnow.

fered small nips of scotch after long, rainy days in the trees; the wood-carver in Dorrigo who transformed old fenceposts into beautiful bowls and taught me to recognize the timbers of my favorite trees; my technician, Wayne Higgins, whose keen eye and steady hand almost never failed to shoot the line over the branch; and the many friends who accompanied me on sampling trips and enthusiastically endured leeches and heights. There were also colorful characters: the thieves who stole a fallen cedar tree out of the national park; the milk-bar (coffee-shop) owners, horrified by my khaki clothes and the machete hanging from my belt, who nonetheless served a terrific milkshake; the counterculture Australians with hallucinogenic aspirations, who continually collected rain-forest fruits and seeds to smoke or otherwise ingest; the human "moth," a rancher

Climbing a giant kapok tree with the single-rope technique. This is the tallest tree I have ever climbed with ropes, in this case to survey epiphytes along the Amazon River in Peru. The village shaman said that if the spirits were willing to allow us to climb this sacred tree, we could; the very first line went up and over the branch, a sign that the spirits looked favorably on our conservation project. Photograph by Phil Wittman.

who ventured into the local pub whenever its light went on; and the occasional tourist who came to the national park in stiletto heels, walked a short distance onto the trail, only to scream "Leeches!!!" and stumble hurriedly back to her car.

After overcoming my initial dilemmas of learning to recognize a rain forest and climbing trees, I selected several long-term study sites in national parks or reserves. At each location I rigged replicate trees for permanent canopy access. The biggest challenge was undoubtedly the giant stinging tree, or gympie-gympie (*Dendrocnide excelsa,* family Urticaceae). This species, as its name implies, has thousands of stinging hairs that coat both leaves and petioles. Its physical hairs can painfully tear the skin, besides which chemical hairs inject a toxin into the freshly scratched surface. In 1908 an Australian chemist named Petrie reported that stinging trees have a toxicity up to thirty-nine times stronger than that of common nettles. Both giant stinging trees and common nettles are in the same plant family (Urticaceae), but nettles grow approximately 3 feet high in fields, whereas stinging trees grow to 200 feet in rain-forest gaps. Because I was interested in longevity and survival as part of leaf growth dynamics, defensive hairs piqued my curiosity.

The Mount Keira Preserve overlooking Wollongong, New South Wales, was suggested to me as an auspicious site for stinging trees. Evidently the slight disturbances (landslides, road-building) on the escarpment created excellent conditions for the growth of this pioneer tree (that is, a tree that colonizes open areas or disturbed sites). Stinging trees grew within the preserve, to 150 feet with a diameter of up to 8 feet, along a trail system built by Boy Scouts who sometimes camped there. Unfortunately, my elation at this discovery was quickly dampened by the Scout caretaker, whose uninvited flirtatious overtures rendered my use of the Scout trails rather uncomfortable and downright risky. To avoid awkward confrontations, I decided to enter the preserve from the opposite side of the mountain and make my own private trail.

After reconnoitering, I found a wonderful gully, where it was likely that no human being had ever ventured. Superb lyrebirds (*Menura superba,* family Menuridae) were in full song when I first trekked through my newfound patch of remnant rain forest. These magnificent passerine birds were one of the unique rewards of working in Australia. Territorial pairs of lyrebirds inhabited most of my field sites, and over the years I was privileged to watch their magnificent courtship displays. Lyrebirds imitated other birds, developing an extensive repertoire of fifteen to twenty different sounds. They often repeated their medleys for long durations (without a breath, it seemed), and their rich and beautiful tones resonated through the forest. Lyrebirds were a constant, treasured companion throughout my years of Australian research. Ironically, the Mount Keira lyrebirds had some unusual imitations in their repertoire: dogs barking, lawn mowers buzzing, and trucks downshifting. These were perhaps a foreboding commentary on the urban development that was fast encroaching on this region.

In my secret gully I selected trees for climbing. In the case of giant stinging trees, I ascended a neighboring tree and reached across (with gloves) to its branches. Each sampling trip without fail resulted in several stings, but I became quite accustomed to this fiery sensation, similar to a bee sting. Even the dead, dried leaf material retained its stinging capacity. My hands almost always bore the resulting red inflammations, which seemed impossible to avoid owing to my continuous sampling schedule.

My methods were relatively simple. I used a waterproof pen to number leaves sequentially on different branches at different heights of different trees, and then returned monthly to monitor growth, damage, coloration, and eventual death. I traced leaf areas to measure insect damage and kept notebooks of information on leaf growth patterns. From these long-term measurements, I quickly accumulated a large database on the growth dynamics of thousands of rain-forest leaves. The ink lasted remarkably well and enabled me to monitor each leaf permanently for as long as it lived.

I also erected litter traps to sample and collect falling leaf material throughout each month of the year. This was a fairly traditional mode of calculating forest biomass by surveying the weight of wood, foliage, and flowers. A litter trap consists of a 1-meter by 1-meter mesh collecting structure, supported by legs of plastic pipe. When I set out to construct my first traps, unanticipated effects of the Australian labor unions caused me considerable stress. First a transport strike occurred. Then followed a summer holiday period of two months, during which it was impossible to obtain the materials I needed. The strength of the Australian labor unions gave them total control over certain aspects of life. These delays taught me one valuable lesson: to plan my research far in advance.

After I finally had the litter traps and climbing trees set up in my secret gully, I ventured forth eagerly after the first month to empty the trap contents and collect my first samples. It was September, early spring on the Australian calendar. Descending into the gully, I was surprised to feel the ground near my feet moving. In my haste I barely missed stepping on an Australian brown snake (*Pseudonaja textilis,* family Elapidae). This extremely venomous species is renowned for its aggressive behavior during the spring nesting season. Moving ahead more cautiously, I was totally overwhelmed by what I saw. The ground was literally swarming with snakes, all of them poisonous species. Such a multitude had obviously assembled to bask in these perfect sun spots . . . Indiana Jones, take note! I delicately tiptoed out of my snake-filled gully and sighed with relief when safely back in the university car. This dangerous predicament forced me to abandon the gully entirely, for all my attention would have been riveted on the ground rather than on the treetops. I eventually managed to find a rain-forest patch on the lower slopes of Mount Keira Preserve with excellent stinging trees to study, but without swarms of snakes or harassment by caretakers.

Levels of herbivory of up to 42 percent leaf-surface-area removal per year were measured in the canopies of these giant stinging trees, despite the apparent defense of stinging hairs. A host-specific chrysomelid beetle (*Hoplostines viridipenis,* family Chrysomelidae) was adapted to chew exclusively on these veritable pincushions. The levels of herbivory were the highest of any Australian rain-forest tree that I measured. How did this species tolerate such significant loss of photosynthetic tissue? And why did such supposed defenses fail

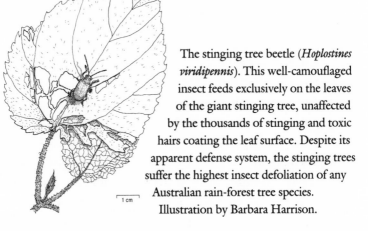

The stinging tree beetle (*Hoplostines viridipennis*). This well-camouflaged insect feeds exclusively on the leaves of the giant stinging tree, unaffected by the thousands of stinging and toxic hairs coating the leaf surface. Despite its apparent defense system, the stinging trees suffer the highest insect defoliation of any Australian rain-forest tree species. Illustration by Barbara Harrison.

to protect the leaves? Apparently the fast growth rate of stinging trees and their relatively low investment in leaf tissue (leaves were thin and short-lived) enabled the trees to replace damaged foliage without dying. And the stinging hairs that were so effective in defending leaves from humans were obviously not effective in deterring beetles. Presumably in Asia, where the Urticaceae family evolved, this mode of plant defense was very successful against mammal predators. I was incredulous, all the same, to realize that, despite the toxic hairs, the stinging trees suffered more insect damage than any other rain-forest tree that I measured. High levels of variability in defoliation among different species was a startling discovery, and led to further study.

My second long-term field site was established at an elevation of 1,700 meters in the cool temperate or montane rain forests of New England National Park in New South Wales. This region of Australia was ironically called New England because a few deciduous trees (oak, maple) thrived in several nearby towns, turning color in the autumn just as they do in my homeland of upstate New York. My field camp in New England National Park was a tiny hut called Tom's Cabin (named after the first ranger of the park, according to local lore, not a legacy of Harriet Beecher Stowe's Uncle Tom, as I had first assumed). It stood at the boundary (or ecotone) of rain forest and wet sclerophyll forest amid a stand of my third study species, Antarctic beech (*Nothofagus moorei,* family Fagaceae). The sun almost never shone on Tom's Cabin. It was a world of mist, moss, fungus, clouds, constant drizzle, and cool air blowing in from the coast onto this east-facing escarpment. Often those cool breezes turned into raging storms; snapping branches and falling trees provided background music as I huddled inside my cabin measuring leaf areas or counting insects. There was no electricity, but the cabin boasted an enormous gas-operated shower, large enough to accommodate a cow (or so claimed the ranger). It was an incredible luxury to return to the cabin after a wet, exhausting day of tree climbing and find the gas bottle full enough to allow a hot shower; it was devastating to arrive and find it empty, which happened more often than I care to remember. Equipped with lanterns, matches, food supplies, and notebooks, Tom's Cabin became my base camp from which I tackled the cool temperate rain-forest canopies. I was even "adopted" by a native tiger cat *(Dasyurus maculatus,* family Dasyuridae), who became tame enough to creep into the cabin and defiantly grab a steak from my fireplace grill. Although I was sorry to sacrifice the steak, it was marvelous to glimpse this unusual marsupial cat at close range.

As a woman working long weeks alone in remote places, I was fortunate to have very few experiences that engendered fear. Locals would occasionally take the wrong road home from the pub and end up pounding raucously on my door, but for the most part the world went on without me when I stayed at Tom's Cabin. Most Australian men probably viewed me as an eccentric. Later I was teased because

my Rockport hiking boots were the ugliest women's shoes my father-in-law had ever seen, or because I was not adept with a pressing
iron (an essential skill for snaring a husband in rural Australia). The
notion of a woman traveling 10,000 miles to a remote continent to
study tree canopies was not only preposterous, but downright suspicious, to most of the Australian men I encountered. To travel even
100 miles to pursue intellectual ideas that had no practical basis in
the kitchen or bedroom may in fact have been laughable to many
rural Australians, male or female. My sojourns in the bush were often lonely. Field research by its nature requires long periods of solitude, first to make observations and collect data, and second to write
up the results. But I found these times alone to be very strengthen-
ing, as they encouraged me to develop confidence in myself.

The cool temperate or cloud forests reminded me superficially of
the temperate deciduous forests of my childhood. Antarctic beech
was related to the American beech of the northern deciduous forests.
In Oceania the cool temperate rain forests were remnants of the
Antarctic rain-forest element that extended from southern Queensland down into Tasmania and New Zealand. They were a fascinating
example of naturally occurring monocultures in nature, with beech
trees occupying approximately 95 percent of cool temperate forest
canopies. (A forest stand with one dominant tree species is called
monodominant.) In New South Wales these pure stands of Antarctic
beech represent a potential feast for a leaf-feeding insect. How can a
tree species that dominates the forest manage to protect itself from
insect epidemics? Does the plant produce toxins to defend itself?
Antarctic beech was my third study species, which enabled me to ask
questions about how monocultures protect themselves from insect
epidemics.

During my years of canopy research from Tom's Cabin, I encountered my first strange case of a UFO (unidentified feeding organism).

In 1979 the Antarctic beeches lost enormous amounts of leaf area to a mysterious herbivore that attacked the foliage for two weeks in October (alas, while I was not present) and then disappeared. What was left was a severely defoliated population of leaves, with no sign of the guilty marauders. In the course of my career I have repeatedly observed evidence of defoliators, then spent hours, weeks, even years to find the responsible munchers. Antarctic beech exhibited a slightly temperate leafing pattern (like its American beech relatives), where approximately half of the leaves emerged every spring (September–October) and half senesced in autumn (April–June). With this massive flush of new foliage, some opportunistic herbivore had adapted its life cycle to invade the beech canopies at the appropriate time and devour the tender new leaves. Every year the beech trees lost more than half of their new foliage from this UFO.

Because of this seasonal pattern, I had to wait a full year after my first observation of the massive defoliation to solve the beech mystery. I was nervous and apprehensive. Obviously, it was possible that the defoliator might not return two years in a row. Perhaps 1979 was part of a cycle that only occurred every twenty-five years and I would never find the culprit. All the same, I packed my gear for a long stay in Tom's Cabin the following spring and built several hardwood ladders that mounted the beech trunks, to facilitate canopy access day or night, rain or shine.

On the first warm evening in late September, I was rewarded for my efforts. Prowling in the canopy with my flashlight, I saw the subtle movements of a few tiny caterpillars, dangling from the young leaves on delicate threads of silk. But I did not observe them feeding on the beech leaves. I returned several successive days, and the numbers of caterpillars virtually exploded until approximately ten larvae occupied each new leaf. And they began feeding! First they ate the uppermost leaf, presumably the most tender and soft, since it was the youngest tissue. As the caterpillars grew a little bigger and their mouthparts became slightly stronger, they ate the next leaf, gradually moving down the branch in lawnmower fashion, growing larger as they fed on successively tougher leaves. I made careful measurements of their abundance and feeding rates. Then, as suddenly as they had arrived, the caterpillars were gone. The new leaves were mere skeletons. I had not managed to collect any larvae to rear and hatch into adults for identification, and the defoliators escaped unidentified. Discouraged, I returned to Sydney to wait yet another year to complete my beech–herbivore saga.

The next year, as predicted, the larvae appeared and repeated their massive defoliation of the new beech foliage. I had time to visit several different stands of beech, and found that some had larvae and some did not. Obviously, the herbivores had not managed to locate all of the available forest patches. When any organism is distributed in patches, rather than in a regular distribution, an element of chance is involved in discovery by a predator. In fact, some scientists believe that a plant scattered in patches throughout a forest may escape herbivores by virtue of its distribution pattern.

This second year I carefully removed some of the larvae and clipped a healthy supply of beech branches to put in large plastic garbage bags. I loaded the car with them and returned to my small flat in Sydney, where my living room became a miniature beech forest. I placed large vats of branches all over the floor and let the larvae munch away until they had passed through several instars (stages of a developing insect between molting). They then underwent metamorphosis, turning into white, crystallized pellets. These small metamorphosed bodies dropped to the floor and emerged two to three weeks later as copper-colored chrysomelid beetles. In the rain forest, the larvae had fallen onto the forest floor and become buried in the humus, which was how they had eluded me. Having now collected all the life phases of my mysterious but important herbivore, I happily took my specimens to the entomologists at the zoology department of the University of Sydney. They could not identify the insect. I took it to the Australian Museum in Sydney, whose entomologists did not recognize it either. I took it to the entomology division of the Commonwealth Scientific and Industrial Research Organization (CSIRO) in Canberra, and experts there could not identify it. They suggested that it might be a new genus of chrysomelid beetle. So, I sent samples to the world expert on chrysomelid beetles, Dr. Brian Selman, at the University of Newcastle-upon-Tyne in Newcastle, England. The quest for the identity of this herbivore had become an international journey.

After several months I was thrilled to receive news that it *was* a new genus of chrysomelid beetle. Brian named it *Nothofagus novacastria,* after the specific host tree of the beetle and after Newcastle (*novacastria* is the latinized version), since he taught at the university of that name in England and the beetle was discovered only a hundred miles north of Newcastle, Australia. Dr. Selman delightedly "cursed" at my discovery, because this new species completely altered his recently published phylogeny of the chrysomelid beetles.

I affectionately named it the gul beetle, as a bicentennial gift to my undergraduate institution, Williams College in Massachusetts. (A latinized version of Williams is *gulielmensian*.) As a mere graduate student, I could not offer the traditional alumni gift of a large monetary bequest, but naming a new species seemed an appropriate contribution for a field biologist.

Although physically nondescript, the beetle had an incredible synchrony with its food plant. It harmonized with seasonal patterns of beech-leaf emergence and exerted an enormous impact on leaf survival in a very short period. The herbivory losses of 51 percent of new beech leaves were extremely high compared to other forests, yet no mortality of beech trees was observed during my twelve years of observations. Nonetheless, twelve years is a very short time in the lifespan of a tree that may live for several thousand years, so the impact of the beetle may not become obvious without several decades of study. Conversely, the beetle populations may fluctuate over several years, with outbreaks (as during the 1980s) interspersed with periods of quiescence. Insect–plant relationships are more complicated than I ever imagined, especially in tall forests where many activities are difficult to observe.

The beech herbivore was not the only mysterious chewer of my research experience. In fact, more often than not, insect herbivores in tree canopies were cryptic either in space (they hid in the foliage or bark) or in time (they appeared only for short periods).

My first two years of research were disappointing in terms of insect discoveries. During most of the time I spent suspended on a rope, I rarely saw insect herbivores in action. This was puzzling, given that the young leaves of most trees were disappearing at annual rates ranging from 15 to 50 percent loss of leaf-surface area. These percentages, four to five times higher than the annual losses reported for most northern temperate deciduous forests, forced me to ask two important questions:

1. Who and where were the herbivores responsible for such voracious feeding?
2. Do all rain-forest canopies suffer equally high herbivory, or was Australia simply different?

The answer to question 2 might take me a lifetime to answer. The answer to question 1 came relatively quickly, by accident.

My warm temperate rain-forest site was Never-Never Land, a remote section of Dorrigo National Park. (As a fan of Peter Pan, I thought this name particularly appropriate for one of my research areas.) One night, taking a midnight stroll to the outhouse, I became aware of loud chewing sounds. With my flashlight, I discovered several walking sticks (family Phasmatodea) busily consuming the young leaves of the calico tree (*Callicoma serratifolia,* family Cunoniaceae). To my amazement and delight, nocturnal feeding was commonplace throughout the forest. This was a breakthrough. Most herbivores fed at night in the rain-forest canopy, rather than by day. I changed my routine to accommodate this discovery; insect spotlighting expeditions became a major part of my research and yielded many exciting discoveries. From these successful night observations, I found that the herbivores in Australian rain-forest canopies were mainly beetles (order Coleoptera), as well as butterfly larvae (order Lepidoptera), grasshoppers (order Orthoptera), and true bugs (order Hemiptera).

In no cases were vertebrates responsible for significant losses of foliage in my Australian rain-forest research (although I encountered them later on other continents). Galahs and parrots occasionally broke off leaves or branches as part of their courtship antics, and tree kangaroos were herbivores but their distribution was limited to small forest patches in far northern Queensland. Koalas were significant herbivorous animals in Australia, but they fed exclusively on eucalypt trees in the dry forests.

To measure and observe leaves and herbivores at night was not difficult in the understory. It proved extremely difficult, however, in the upper canopy. Most of my fieldwork relied upon the use of single-rope technique (SRT) that facilitated vertical access into single trees, and single ropes were easily transported from tree to tree. Climbing trees as part of one's career sounded like a child's dream, but the logistics of ropes in a dense forest were challenging. To rig trees for access to tall canopies required the adept use of a slingshot. Because slingshots were classified as illegal weapons, I made my first model by forming a metal rod into a Y-shape. Many memorable days were spent in the rain forest with fellow students, attempting to shoot fishlines over nearly impossible-to-reach canopy branches. The system required two persons, one to fire a round lead weight from the slingshot and the other to hold onto the reel of fishline attached to the weight. Our conversations verged on the ridiculous—how to identify good crotches, how to aim our balls into those crotches—and were often laced with expletives because trying to aim accurately could be frustrating work. Branches were often higher than they appeared; vines seemed to reach out and grab the fishline, rendering it twisted and permanently stuck; fish sinkers broke free of the line and went sailing off into the unknown; and sometimes the line lodged on the tip of a branch but simply would not slide down into the safety of the crotch. Once the fish line was hoisted over a strong branch and situated in its crotch, I would pull a nylon cord into position to serve as a permanent guide to hoist the climbing rope. I never left my climbing rope in a tree overnight because of the dangers of nibbling rodents, voracious ants and termites, or the weathering effects of sun and rain. My life literally depended on the integrity of the climbing rope.

Limited canopy sampling was accomplished with shotguns, but that type of sampling was destructive and had limited application for my work. I obtained branch samples with shotguns on several occasions when we required flowers from the uppermost canopy, but my shoulder would become badly bruised from the recoil. I contemplated the use of a tree bicycle for access, after watching Al Gentry (a botanist of international repute who tragically died in an airplane crash in Ecuador in 1994) utilize his unique gadget to sample canopy flowers in North Queensland, Australia. The bicycle was ideal for vertical trunks without branches and allowed Al to reach fruits and flowers for his taxonomic studies, but it had limited application for my ecological sampling.

Working alone in a rain-forest canopy was often a detriment. With only one pair of hands and eyes, I could never hope to see all of the herbivores, nor could I sample all of the important leaf populations during relatively short climbs. Over the years my solo efforts were supplemented by volunteers. An innovative organization called Earthwatch promotes research by recruiting volunteers to assist scientists in the field. My first Earthwatch volunteers joined me on expeditions in 1980, and over the next decade more than two hundred fifty of them inspired and enhanced my canopy-research efforts. With Earthwatchers I was able to sample many more leaves and insects. An *espirit de corps* developed that made the work both stimulating and memorable.

During my first Earthwatch expedition in Australia, one canopy episode stands out particularly. On our first night of sampling in the forest, I had asked eleven team members to meet me at the base of a large sassafras (*Doryphora sassafras,* family Monimiaceae), where we planned to hoist light traps to compare moth populations in the upper and lower canopies. (Sassafras, with its evergreen waxy leaves and its widespread distribution throughout all types of Australian forest, was my fourth species of intensive study.) We reached our dark, damp meeting place and I began to explain to my neophyte volunteers how the light traps worked and what we hoped to capture. Suddenly, a thunderous explosion erupted overhead and the entire tree appeared to fly off. About twenty-five brush turkeys (*Alectura lathami,* family Megapodiidae) were roosting in the canopy, and we had unwittingly disturbed them with our flashlights and noisy conversation. Unfortunately for us, brush turkeys defecate heavily when frightened, so both feathers and poop rained down. Everyone stood silent, shocked, and smelly. They quietly returned to their rooms to shower, leaving me worried that I had squelched forever their enthusiasm for science. But the following evening they all showed up for our second light-trap session, with bath towels and rain ponchos triumphantly pinned over their heads and shoulders.

During that same fateful expedition, one of my Earthwatch volunteers panicked during a routine tree-climbing exercise. At the very top of a sassafras tree, Vikki got a rope wedged into her Jumar and its teeth simply would not release. We said prayers and sent a Swiss army knife up the rope. Needless to say, it was one of my more anxious moments: would she cut the correct rope? Wayne Higgins, my technical assistant, heroically talked her down the tree, providing inch-by-inch instruction on how she should manipulate out of her precarious situation. To this day, she writes and reminds me that this experience was one of the most exhilarating of her entire life, even above and beyond her vocation of flying air force jets.

Earthwatchers continued to make significant contributions of time and energy to my canopy research in Australia and elsewhere. I now serve on their board of advisors and am honored to promote the mission of this remarkable organization.

I also sought assistance from fellow students at the University of Sydney. Several others were pursuing fieldwork at remote sites, so we often took turns accompanying one another on research trips. I had many interesting weeks at One Tree Island on the Great Barrier Reef, assisting with student projects on the respiration of coral-cay shrubs, butterfly-fish population dynamics on patch reefs, and plankton in the water column. I even volunteered to capture and mark sea snakes, reputedly the most venomous reptiles in the world, on some remote cays of the Great Barrier Reef—although I must confess that sea snake research definitely stretched my definition of sensible science (see Chapter 3). In return, I gained assistants for tree rigging and climbing, for leaf measurement, for site surveys, and simply for help driving between my far-flung rain-forest patches.

One Earthwatch volunteer from Tennessee kindly sent me a wonderful American slingshot, after he had struggled to rig tall trees in Queensland with my homemade model. (It was easier to obtain a gun in the bush than a slingshot.) When this unsolicited gift arrived at customs in Sydney, I got a call from the police saying that they had confiscated a package for me containing an illegal product. After several months of filling out permit applications and explaining that this weapon was required for my scientific research, the package was released and sent on to me. But the customs officers may have had the last laugh. Inside was not only a slingshot, but also a set of camouflage underwear and a bottle of perfume. This volunteer could not resist sending me the latest elegant lingerie for the jungle. (My Earthwatchers teased me about being a fashion plate, since I wore only khaki clothes, and there had been many jokes about whether my undergarments were also camouflaged.) Because my technician, Wayne, had become engaged just prior to assisting me on this expedition, the same volunteer also sent a gift of perfume for his fiancée. To this day I speculate that my name is listed in Sydney customs records as a scientist of ill repute, whose forest activities are suspicious.

The new slingshot not only made my tree rigging much more accurate, but it also enticed male colleagues to accompany me on field trips for the thrill of using this marvelous "boytoy." I must confess that no female colleagues ever voiced an interest in my unique research tool, but I was the envy of many Australian *cockies* (farmers), who begged to use my slingshot for the troublesome rabbits and foxes on their "stations."

One of my principal field sites in Queensland adjoined a rain-forest lodge, owned and operated by the O'Reilly family. Over the years they became a second family to me, and we shared our love and knowledge of rain-forest natural history. After many seasons of climbing, I had become frustrated with the limitations of ropes; they offered vertical access up a tree but very little horizontal reach. Using local resources and relying on my encouragement, the O'Reillys constructed a canopy walkway — the world's first, to my knowledge — for both ecotourism and research. This new mode of access vastly expanded my horizons for study and also enhanced the experience for guest-house visitors. The walkway facilitated sampling over long periods of time, at night, during storms, and it enabled groups to work collectively in the canopy.

The simplicity of a walkway structure, its low impact on the environment, its safety record, and its ease of access remain unsurpassed for canopy work. Several years later, its effectiveness inspired me to create a series of walkways throughout the world (see Chapter 5). Over a period of ten years, I explored the canopy adjacent to the walkway with hundreds of students and Earthwatch volunteers. Without the risks of ropes, the volunteers were able to develop a sense of wonder for this high frontier. Since the installation of the walkway in 1985, the O'Reillys have also enabled many thousands of tourists to discover the rain-forest canopy. To this day, the O'Reillys are a special part of my international family of canopy enthusiasts, and their lodge remains a center for canopy research.

My fifth rain-forest canopy tree species was the red cedar (*Toona ciliata*, family Meliaceae), selected for study because of its economic importance as Australia's most desirable timber. Cedar trees also serve as important incentives for forest conservation in Australia, which prompted me to document the relationship between these trees and their insect pests. The quest for red cedar during the early 1900s was the major cause of the destruction of Australian rain forests, and this species also suffered massive defoliation from an outbreak insect called the tip moth. I became renowned among the Australian men of my district for my special knowledge of cedar trees. In describing my studies of cedar and the tip moth to the local

Rotary club, they misunderstood my interest to be in the "tit" moth instead of the "tip" moth. I never lived that down and frequently got inquiries from passersby on the streets of my rural town about the status of the tit moths!

I lived in Australia for twelve years, from 1978 to 1990. During that time, I devoted five years to the exclusive study of rain-forest canopies as part of my doctoral research, then juggled pursuits of dry forests, motherhood, and wifely duties (not in that order of importance, however). The opportunity to visit my rain-forest field sites for over a decade (and even longer, since I continue to return every year) provided a valuable opportunity to observe long-term patterns of plant–insect relationships.

It was commonly assumed that rain forests comprised mostly evergreen leaves that lived for one to three years. This generalization has since been revised, based in part upon my long-term measurements, which indicated that some leaves (for instance, shade leaves of sassafras) lived as long as fifteen years. In contrast, leaves on the same sassafras tree lived only two to three years in the sunny, windy environment of the canopy. The patterns of leafing varied widely and included intermittent (leaves flushed throughout the year, but with pulses), continuous (leaves flushed during every month of the year), seasonal (leaves flushed during a specific season), and deciduous (all leaves fell for a period each year) phenology. Insect herbivores often fed exclusively at night, and most leaves suffered more damage when they were young (that is, soft and less toxic) than later in their lives. Despite the boredom that can ensue from repetitious, long-term sampling, such data sets become invaluable over time because they reveal patterns that are not obvious from shorter spans.

2 Life in the Outback

*T*he bush ethos which grew up from making a virtue out of loneliness and hardship built on the stoic virtues of convict Australia. Settled life and domesticity were soft and demoralizing. A "real man" despised comfort and scorned the expression of emotion. . . . Disaster could strike swiftly — some little-understood disease might wipe out the investment in the flock or the herd; a man or a child could die from snakebite, a tetanus-infected wound, a fall from a horse. Or disaster could set in slowly with the onset of drought. It was ever-present and a woman at home alone all day had time to think about it.

—Jill Ker Conway, *The Road from Coorain,* 1990

As a result of my graduate work in rain forests, I was probably the only person in Australia in the early 1980s with any firsthand scientific expertise in tree canopies. This unique qualification led me straight into a postdoctoral opportunity to tackle an ecological problem of enormous economic and emotional magnitude. Many of the trees in rural Australia were dying. Even worse, the mysterious malady was striking the country's dominant forest vegetation, gum trees (Eucalyptus sp., family Myrtaceae). Gum trees were a national symbol of Australia, featured throughout literature and history as well as biology. Numbering more than five hundred species and constituting 95 percent of the tree cover in this dry country, they were undergoing an epidemic that rendered their canopies leafless and ultimately dead. The syndrome, called eucalypt dieback, was afflicting millions of trees by the mid-1980s, with no end in sight. What was causing the dieback? How could landowners reverse this serious degradation of the landscape? And why was it most severe in the rural outback regions, where trees were already sparse? These questions became the focus of my postdoctoral research, and of subsequent years. Because the dieback syndrome appeared to originate in the crowns of the gum trees, I used the canopy-access skills I had acquired in the rain forest to solve it. The challenge of addressing an applied scientific problem led me into ecological complexities that I had never imagined and, on a personal level, into emotional complexities pertaining to marriage and motherhood.

The eucalypt dieback syndrome first entered the literature in 1878, when a farmer named A. Norton wrote in his diary, "I have seen some thousands of acres, chiefly in the New England district of New South Wales, where a plague seems to have carried death through the forest" (*Proceedings of the Royal Society of Queensland,* vol. 3). Over the next hundred years, dieback outbreaks occurred without apparent regularity throughout Australia, striking the jarrah forests (*Eucalyptus marginata,* family Myrtaceae) of Western Australia, the peppermints

(*E. nova-anglica,* family Myrtaceae) of central New South Wales, and even the gray ironbark (*E. drepanophylla,* family Myrtaceae) up in Queensland. These periodic outbreaks were mentioned throughout the settlement of outback Australia, but during the 1980s the dieback syndrome reached epidemic proportions.

Because it appeared most severe in rural landscapes, I moved from the urban center of Sydney to a bush town called Armidale in central New South Wales to study this mysterious environmental disaster. Armidale boasted the only rural-based university in Australia, and at the University of New England I interacted with agricultural scientists as well as a handful of ecologists who also studied the bush. I received a grant from the Australian federal government to examine the possible links between insect outbreaks and tree health of the rural eucalypts.

After Sydney, rural Australia was like a different country. Even the accents and the vocabulary were different. Many "properties" (ranches or farms) had been settled over five generations ago as part of a system whereby settlers were granted ownership of a block of land if they cleared it and built a dwelling there. These early settlers faced extraordinary environmental conditions on their newfound, isolated properties. Drought, winds, floods, disease, clay soils, snakes, insect epidemics, rabbit plagues, and the difficulty of clearing trees were but a few of the challenges. As a result, the graziers developed very stoic attitudes, albeit strong allegiance to their land and livestock.

Visitors entering the New England district of New South Wales were greeted by billboards proclaiming the area as "Glorious New England," a description that in time past had been apt and accurate. Now, beyond these billboards lay a landscape that was stark and dead. The muted, delicate colors of the Australian scrub had given way to the white skeletons of dead gum trees, their bare branches raised toward the sky as if in acceptance of untimely defeat. Sheep huddled beneath trees that could no longer cast shade. The landscape was harsh and barren. The New England district was one of the centers of widespread dieback. Other major areas included Western Australia, southeastern Queensland, and the Australian Capital Territory. The symptoms were obvious: tree crowns in varying stages of stress, decline, and mortality.

The dieback seemed complex, with no single factor correlated to the perplexing malady. Only one characteristic stood out: the trees were afflicted in their upper crowns first, with death of the lower branches occurring shortly thereafter. Dieback was perhaps best defined by its observed symptoms. First, the tree declined in vigor and its crown thinned out at the tips of the twigs, then along the branches toward the trunk. As the outer portions of the tree died, the dead branches protruded beyond the remaining foliage. After considerable decline of the outer crown, new shoots flushed from the trunk and main branches. These shoots, called epicormic branches or coppicing, represented a last effort on the part of the tree to produce foliage and photosynthesize. Sometimes the trees exhibited a healthy recovery, but more often they perished. Usually several cycles of epicormic shoots took place, each one progressively shorter, as the tree declined and finally died. Eucalypts appeared to have incredible energy reserves, enabling them to flush several times after complete defoliation. Once those reserves were depleted by successive sprouting, however, the trees entered the final, irreversible phase of the dieback syndrome.

As a young graduate student, I had previously approached research solely with an academic curiosity. Now I was heartened to tackle an applied ecological problem. The fact that thousands of acres of landscape, and millions of dollars of tourism and agriculture, were linked to the dieback syndrome heightened the urgency for me to succeed in finding the cause. I was also forced to adapt my scientific writing style for the public, since there were demands by the media to address dieback on television and in the popular literature. Sometimes my research created controversy; those who championed environmental causes in rural Australia were termed *greenies,* a label with a negative connotation. I had to walk a fine line between the rural landowners, who were suspicious of scientists, and the scientific community, which mistrusted the farmers. As a farmer's wife, I found it a delicate balance — yet the stakes were high.

Many factors were implicated in the eucalypt dieback syndrome, including biological conditions, human impacts, physical factors, or a combination thereof. Suspected agents included insect defoliators, fungal diseases, drought, alteration of water tables, nutrient imbalances in the soil caused by application of fertilizers, soil erosion, reduced soil aeration due to compaction by the hooves of grazing livestock, clearing of land, overstocking of cattle or sheep, and salinity. Even overconsumption of eucalypt leaves by "Billy Bluegum" (Australian slang for a koala) was listed as a causal agent.

Probably no single factor was responsible for dieback, but rather a complex synergism. Unfortunately, interactions are often difficult to unravel. For example, a drought may stress certain species of trees, then is followed by insect attack, then by recovery of some trees but reduced soil aeration for others, and perhaps repeated defoliation. The result would be patchy dieback within a region. Even more complicated was the possibility that a particular level of insect attack in drought years might have a very different effect on the health of trees than the same amount in wetter years. As with many biological problems, one year of study could not solve a multifaceted malady of long-lived organisms such as trees.

My colleague in this project, Harold (Hal) Heatwole (professor of zoology at the University of New England), soon realized that few scientists had tackled this serious ecological problem simply because it was so complex. In the scientific community, it is often difficult to obtain funding for a multifaceted problem because it is impossible to conceptualize the research with a single well-structured hypothesis. In the course of our research, Hal and I wore many hats in addition to our respective scientific specialties of herpetology and plant ecology. We dabbled in mycology, soil science, dendrology, meteorology, agronomy, ornithology, and even climatology. For me this research was probably a turning point, in that it forced me to address global issues of forest conservation and the human impact on ecosystems. It also taught me that if we are to be effective stewards of our environment, we need to develop unambiguous communication about science to the public.

Many graziers, who were skillful readers of the landscape as they watched their sheep or cattle, claimed that the leaves of the dying gum trees were eaten by herbivores. Suspects included koalas (who frequently sat in a single tree and denuded it over a short time), insects (several species of beetles were observed to undergo periodic outbreaks), or an unknown fungal pathogen. In Western Australia the government spent millions of dollars to study regional dieback, and a root pathogen was eventually uncovered as the principal cause of mortality in that state. *Phytophthora cinnamomi,* a fungus unknowingly introduced via the soil of tractor tires from Malaysian avocado farms, had infested the jarrah forests of Western Australia and killed almost every stand. In eastern Australia no such pathogen had been isolated, nor had any other sole suspect, when we initiated fieldwork in 1983.

Our first task was to ascertain whether or not the foliage was being consumed (as hypothesized by many farmers) or was simply falling off as a consequence of stress from other causes. I set up climbing sites (similar to those in my rain-forest project) in patches of dry forest and stands of gum trees. A series of healthy and un-healthy tree stands were located, and replicate canopies were mea-sured for levels of defoliation at each site. Low-level, middle-level, and high-level branches were permanently numbered with my trusty waterproof marking pens, and I returned monthly to measure the ar-eas of leaf surface consumed. I found that gum leaves lived approxi-mately two years, a significantly shorter time than the fifteen-year-old sassafras leaves I had measured in the understory of the rain forest. Because of this relatively short lifespan, it was possible to monitor at least two flushes of eucalypt leaves over the duration of our five-year grant.

The results were shocking. Herbivory in eucalypt trees was significantly more pronounced than in any other trees I had mea-sured, and higher than documented in previous records in the scientific literature. The insect attacks were also extremely variable, ranging from negligible on some trees to total defoliation else-where. In some cases insects ate the entire crown of a gum tree within a period of several weeks. Because eucalypts are evergreen, they flushed again after defoliation; sometimes the second flush was also eaten, and even a third.

I conducted experiments to prevent insects from eating foliage, by applying insecticide very carefully to some portions of canopy and comparing the growth there with that in a control area that had not been sprayed. It came as no surprise that the branches without in-sects grew bigger and had more leaf-surface area than the branches with insects.

To our amazement, these high levels of stress did not always kill the eucalypts. Herbivory was correlated with tree mortality in many instances, but not all. We had only half solved the dieback dilemma. It turned out that human impacts also constituted an important, al-beit complex, causal agent.

Many human impacts had severely altered the Australian landscape over the past hundred years and were implicated in the dieback. These changes included intensive clearing of much of the woodland, the trampling of grazing animals (mainly sheep, but also cattle), the introduction of European grasses that provided better fodder during winter, the addition of superphosphate fertilizers to the soil to encourage growth of the introduced grasses, the reduction in abundance of native grasses as well as the organisms they supported, and the decrease in native birds that had roosted in the trees before widespread clearing.

Each of these changes had a far-reaching impact on the natural conditions. For example, the introduction of sheep and cattle resulted in different patterns of trampling of the soil, differential consumption of plant material, different nutrient cycling back into the soil via defecation, and even altered grazing pressures on the pastures owing to the gregarious feeding habits of flocks of sheep. Although livestock was extremely important as the economic backbone of Australia, these animals degraded the natural landscape by their sheer numbers and the fact that their grazing habits differed from those of the native herbivores (kangaroos and wallabies). Worse, the sheep (and rabbits, another human-introduced economic disaster) also nibbled on eucalypt seedlings, thereby preventing regeneration.

In the course of my research in rural Australia, I met many farmers in the district because our study sites were situated in their pasturelands. I suppose that, at age twenty-nine, my biological clock was ticking rather loudly. Through our mutual interest in dead trees, I met a local grazier and married him at the ripe old age of thirty. It seemed to be a match made in heaven: I was a scientist looking for pastures with stands of eucalypts that exhibited dieback; Andrew was a grazier with five thousand acres of pasture, many with patches of trees in different stages of decline. He was energetic, enthusiastic, and full of Australian charm . . . and a bachelor in this rural district where the population included very few eligible women.

Most of our so-called dates were visits to his farm, where I assisted with sheep, cattle, and even painting a trailer. But love is blind (or is it age-related hormones?), and I did not notice the absence of flowers, jewelry, movie dates, and other more conventional courtship rituals. When I was offered a job in Puerto Rico, I asked Andrew if he would accompany me for a sabbatical year to the other side of the globe, so that I could have a turn at my career choice before settling on the farm. He resolutely declared that he had promised his father that he would spend the rest of his life on the farm, having just left a career stint in Canberra, the nation's capital. I perhaps should have been wary, in that we had absolutely no discussion of compromise on this matter; but at the time, my loyalty transcended all else.

Ironically, I had a climbing mishap during our courtship that may have influenced my decision to wed without further discussion of my possible career aspirations. One afternoon as heavy thunderclouds were rolling in, I senselessly decided to climb a gum tree to complete my monthly sampling before the storm. I knew better than to rush, or to climb without a buddy; so what happened is entirely a consequence of my own disregard for safety. Standing on a branch, I slipped while changing from my ascender (Jumar) to my descender (whales-tail), and I fell the 15 feet from my last sample branch to the rough pasture. Fortunately, nothing was broken (except my confidence), although I suffered painful bruises. To this day I suspect that this accident at a critical time in my life may have affected my judgment. Did it convince me to seek the safety of marriage and housewifery rather than the challenges of an unconventional career in some remote jungle of the world? Would my decision have been different if I had had women mentors in Australian academia to advise me? Like dieback, the emotional choices of women in midlife and in midcareer are complex and impossible to link to a single explanation.

Regardless of the reasons, with the notion of creating a research laboratory in our backyard, I naively married a grazier in rural Australia. My mother cried when she heard the news. What level-headed daughter would choose to remain in the outback of Australia, 10,000 miles away from the comforts of her childhood and an ocean away from her friends and family? Like my initial approach to a doctoral thesis, my view of marriage was romantic, and executed without women colleagues available locally for discussions of the heart. I entered into marriage with good faith that my husband and I would compromise on issues of career and family. Only after several years did I realize how large that ocean was and how enormous — though subtle — those cultural differences were.

My decision to stay in Australia was significant not only for my personal life but also for my career. Rather than finish my postdoctoral project and move into the permanent job that had been offered me in Puerto Rico, I extended my postdoctoral post in order to continue working on tree declines. I needed to convey this decision to my colleague Hal, who was departing for three months' research in Antarctica on the very day I accepted Andrew's marriage proposal. I hastened to the local airport, arriving just before his departure and rushed to give him a big hug. Hal was usually a very affectionate and warm person, so I was shocked when he recoiled in horror. He quickly pulled me into a corner and whispered that he had a red-bellied black snake (*Pseudechis porphyriacus,* family Elapidae) coiled around his neck, in transit to Sydney for a colleague. By literally hugging a venomous snake, I could have suffered a fatal bite. He laughed uproariously and I laughed nervously. Never again shall I hug a herpetologist without prior permission! Hal was delighted with my news, and we both rejoiced at the notion of continuing our dieback research.

My 5,000-acre research laboratory was a marvelous mixture of rocky pastures, manicured grazing paddocks, and patches of sclerophyll woodlands. Our property was called Ruby Hills, evidently named after the discovery of garnets in the surrounding hills (although I romanticized that the name also came from the wonderful reddish color of summer sunsets over the pastures). I loved the isolation, which included many days of total solitude except for the raucous sounds of choughs (birds that looks like crows) and magpies. I cooked, sewed, wrote, and observed in the dry woodlands. I conducted experiments on insect exclusion on saplings and experimented with regeneration of native and nonnative tree species. I fought drought, rabbits, and fire, watching some of my favorite trees succumb to the natural — and unnatural — disasters of "life on the land."

My first real home as a married woman was a former station hand's cottage. Andrew used to call it a real estate agent's dream — full of potential, almost all of it unrealized. In a layperson's terms, that meant *rough*. Fortunately, the bathroom was plumbed, but its undulating linoleum floor was unbelievably cold in winter. (Unlike coastal Australia, we had many months of cold and even snow, as we were perched on top of the Great Dividing Range at an elevation of 4,500 feet.) Other unique features included orange kitchen cabinets, a screened-in meat room adjacent to the carport (originally built to hang carcasses of lamb or beef), and a definite spartan appeal (no central heating, no air-conditioning, no dishwasher, no curtains, no closets, no attic, no basement, no light fixtures other than bare bulbs.) On a positive note, we had what many other young married couples did not have: a 300-foot driveway, a 100-acre backyard, a large dog kennel, a shearing shed, a constant breeze blowing through the floorboards, and an army of blowflies guarding the back door. We delighted in the positive features and laughed about the rest. The isolated location offered me ample opportunity to sit alone and write grants or analyze data, those important elements in the life of a scientist that are rarely acknowledged. I expended a lot of elbow grease making our first home livable and lovable — stripping and varnishing floors, painting, installing light fixtures, wallpapering, making curtains and pillows, and creating decorations out of odds and ends. I had a strong nesting instinct and a lot of optimism and energy to try to convert this cottage into a pastoral palace.

Our nearest town, Walcha (aboriginal for *watering hole*), was 10 miles down the road. It boasted four pubs, one grocery store, one post office, one pharmacy, three banks, and three stock-and-station agencies (where graziers organize to sell wool, buy sheep chemicals or other rural supplies, and learn about what the neighbors are doing). Banks were important for borrowing and/or depositing money, depending on the weather and the market, and pubs were important for celebrations or sorrows of the rural economy. My grazier husband claimed that these two institutions, the banks and the pubs, were the main pillars of a rural town. The hospital had fifty-four beds and one full-time doctor. Both of my children were delivered there by the general practitioner, in whom I had utmost confidence despite an absence of technological trappings. During my eight years in Walcha, I met many wonderful people whose friendships I will treasure all my life.

During the first weeks of our marriage, I was awakened one night by gunshots outside the window. Anxious to protect his bride, Andrew leapt out of bed and rushed off in the truck to chase the culprits. To his chagrin, he jumped into his truck wearing only his underdaks, as Australian men call their underwear. Evidently, when he finally caught up with the assailants, he could not without great humiliation get out of his truck to confront them. It turned out that the gunshots were fired by dingo hunters or foxhunters, who were poaching. Through some slight leak at the local pub, this story of the naked poacher-roundup circulated in no time. I quickly learned that the bush telegraph (an affectionate term for the circulation of gossip) was extremely effective in our rural district.

When I washed dishes in my kitchen, I looked out past our small fenced garden to a vast pastoral expanse. Despite the constant winds and dry spells that sometimes seemed interminable, I loved this dynamic rural landscape. Changes included the subtle color shifts from brown to tan to green grass, depending on the amount of rain; the presence or absence of sheep, from rare moments of quiet to incessant bleating during spring lambing; clear versus smoky horizons, depending on bush fires; the extremes of sultry heat waves versus frosty mornings; and even the daily shifts from sunrise to sunset.

One of my constant companions was Jock, a satin bowerbird (*Ptilonorhynchus violaceus,* Family Paradisaeidae) who seemed determined to find a mate in our garden. These birds construct a courtship display area, called a bower, from sticks adorned with blue objects, in order to woo their mates. Sometimes called the playboys of the forest, bowerbirds are usually restricted to rain forests and their edges. There they find natural blue objects (flowers, berries) to decorate their courtship bowers. In this case, Jock had discovered his very own cache of blue objects: our clothespins, several pieces of Lego, and blue plastic straws rescued from the trash. I have seen bowers in the Queensland rain forests adorned with Fosters' beer cans (also blue), a sad legacy of nature's adapting to human habits.

Even as a newlywed, I continued my dieback research on a full-time basis. My husband and I had utmost respect and enthusiasm for each other's vocation. (It was only later, after children entered the scene, that this lovely respect was broken down irrevocably by out-

The satin bowerbird, playboy of the Australian rain forest. He displays a collection of blue objects, including clothespins, shells, flowers, and plastic toys such as Legos, to attract a mate into his bower made of twigs. The bowerbird was my constant companion throughout eleven years of canopy research in Australian forests. Illustration by Barbara Harrison.

side forces.) Our farm was situated approximately one hour's drive from the university. This distance was very manageable on the quiet country roads, and I economized on my driving time by spending long days in the university's laboratories and library (plus grocery shopping), interspersed with long days at home in my field laboratory or writing (plus housewifery) in our remote cottage. I was thrilled to waken one morning to the sounds of a koala munching on the leaves of a ribbon gum (*Eucalyptus viminalis,* family Myrtaceae) directly outside our front door. I was actually able to climb the tree and pat the dear creature on its bottom, because it was so lethargic and uninterested in anything but gum leaves.

The koala was an innocent victim of the dieback syndrome. Many farmers had observed koalas in local trees, and also noted that the trees were dying. Because koalas consume foliage, it was logical to assume that perhaps they were responsible for tree mortality. But this was not the case. Koalas were not abundant, but their distribution was fairly uneven throughout the New England tablelands. In addition, they fed on only six to eight species of the five hundred fifty or more eucalypts that existed. Stories circulated about rural groups who half jokingly suggested establishing koala bounties, to save the trees. However, our measurements of eucalypt herbivory showed unequivocally that insects were the major foliage feeders and that koalas almost never caused the death of a tree. Still, the role of koalas in dieback created great controversy. It was difficult to know which organism, the gum tree or the koala, was more revered in Australian tradition. Both were "fair dinkum" symbols of rural Australia, so any allegations against either icon created much local outcry. I was relieved that koalas were not responsible for dieback; otherwise, I think Australians might have preferred dead trees to taking drastic measures to reduce koala populations.

After three summers of foliage measurement in eucalypt canopies, Hal and I had enough data to forge a compelling link between the insects and the dieback. The Australian equivalent of the American June bug is most active in summer; but since that involves December (not June) in Australia, the insect is aptly named the Christmas beetle (*Anoplognathes* sp., family Scarabidae, order Coleoptera). Every summer these herbivores emerged from their larval stage in the soil (where we suspect they ate roots) and fed gregariously on the gum leaves. Many nights I literally could not sleep because of the sounds of millions of chewing beetles. It was deafening.

Ironically, many human alterations to the landscape (for instance, the introduction of nonnative grasses, and livestock trampling the soil around shade trees) created conditions that actually promoted the survival of the beetle larvae. Not only were fewer trees left for

The Christmas beetle (*Anoplognathes* sp.), a voracious insect that has defoliated millions of eucalypt trees in eastern Australia. Its survival has been enhanced by agricultural practices. Illustration by Barbara Harrison.

Anoplognathus

1 inch

these voracious herbivores, thereby concentrating their numbers, but their young were surviving in greater proportions. Over time the outbreaks of Christmas beetles became more severe. I recorded the annual consumption of over 300 percent leaf-surface area by these beetles; that is, three successive leaf flushes were eaten in some trees during one year. When this damage was compounded by intermittent drought, increased soil erosion, and other factors, the synergism with beetles resulted in severe decline of trees. In essence, the beetles were the last straw in a series of environmental perturbations that stressed even the most robust trees beyond recovery.

Life on the land was fraught with ups and downs. There was an Australian notion that farmers were never content unless they were complaining: either it rained too often or too seldom, there was too much grass or too little, too much (taxable) money derived from wool sales or not enough, the lambs were too large or too small. Obviously, to endure the hardships of Australia's physical climate, these landowners had to be very stoic, and their attitudes adjusted accordingly. I had great respect for the optimism and fortitude that my husband showed toward his profession of raising sheep and cattle.

We were married in 1983, during the worst drought in twenty-five years. The day after our wedding, the drought broke and it poured rain throughout our honeymoon on Lord Howe Island, just off the east coast of Australia. I shall never forget the small plane in which we rode to Lord Howe in the midst of gale-force winds and heavy rain; even the pilot was saying prayers. Upon our arrival at the island, it continued to rain. We snorkeled in the rain, rode bikes in the rain, hiked in the rain — I confess that it was extremely disappointing. But my grazier husband, imbued with an outback philosophy, rejoiced at the rain and looked forward to returning home to watch the grass grow.

Regardless of weather, the rural population was dedicated to weddings, christenings, and the annual horse races. Every year in our district, a special race day called the Geebungs took place. The Geebungs were in essence an excuse for the district to picnic and drink together, ostensibly to watch the racing — but we knew otherwise. Betting was capped at fifty cents, and the races themselves were often ignored by the majority of the crowd. People brought lavish picnics with champagne and chicken, and the women modeled their best hats and dresses. Baby carriages were a must. (In our district, breeding was perhaps a woman's most important achievement.) The "blokes" drank beer and talked about the wool market and the weather. The "sheilas" usually drank wine (often called Chateau Cardboard by the middle class, who served it from one-gallon cardboard boxes with a plastic spout) and talked about babies and how the men overworked.

Andrew and I enjoyed the Geebungs. We shared the company of other young friends whom we rarely saw during the busy months of activities focused on livestock (or, in my oddball case, research). I was always amazed at the conditions of this annual festivity. We sat in the middle of a grassy field next to a dusty racetrack and a dilapidated shed. Drinks were sold in plastic cups, and our picnics were always accompanied by millions of "blowies," or flies (*Lucilia cuprina,* family Calliphoridae, order Diptera). The act of swatting flies away from one's face was jokingly referred to as the Australian Salute. We all engaged in serious renditions of this hand waving as we tried to keep these Diptera out of our drinks and our chicken. I am sure my digestive tract is much more robust as a result of inadvertent consumption of blowflies. The flies in the Australian outback were among the most tenacious pests I have ever encountered. They not only infested every roast I cooked, but they also resulted in the widespread death of sheep. The blowflies invaded any wound or unhygienic region (such as the nether parts) on a sheep and laid their eggs there. Upon hatching, the larvae fed on the flesh of the animal, rapidly killing it unless treated with strong chemicals. This cause of sheep mortality was one of the most common, and certainly the most grotesque. Australian geneticists were attempting to breed strains of merino sheep with greater resistance to blowfly attack, for both hygienic and economic reasons.

Flies were not just a nuisance to sheep. Within the home they infested babies, food, and even damp clothes or towels. If meat were left uncovered on the kitchen counter, it often became a future hatching site for maggots. The following notation was written in 1844 by Mrs. Charles Meredith ("Notes and Sketches of New South Wales"):

Blowies Cause a Stir
Flies are another nuisance; they swarm in every room in tens of thousands, and black the breakfast or dinner table as soon as the viands appear, tumbling into the cream, tea, wine, and gravy with the most disgusting familiarity.

Flies also permeated the Australian vocabulary. Many colorful expressions originated from flies: "drink with the flies," to drink alone; "blow-in," an uninvited guest; "lively as a blowfly on a winter's day," a lethargic employee (to name but a few). In general, Australians were not affectionate about many creatures on the landscape. *Bities* was the common term for a large proportion of Australian wildlife: spiders, bull-ants, scorpions, flies, bluebottle jellyfish, mosquitoes, or any biting creatures. Other animals featured colorfully in rural slang: "emu's breakfast" was a jocular expression meaning a drink and a good look around; "stone the bloody crows" was an expression of amazement; a "frilled lizard" was a man with a whisker-framed face; "has a death adder in his pocket" implies stingy; and "sparrow's fart" means just before dawn. The bush language is rich and full of wonderful imagery.

In the midst of drought, fire, blowfly infection of sheep, and unpredictable changes in the world market for wool, my Australian spouse and his father worked together tending to maintenance of the flock. It was primarily a man's role to round up, count, inspect, drench (apply antibiotics), and shear the sheep. Women usually managed the domestic responsibilities: cooking, sewing, housework, shopping, and babies. On our ranch sheep numbered as few as five thousand (during winter) and as many as fifteen thousand (just after lambing in early spring). And, always, new ideas plus old problems demanded attention. One year we experimented with coats for the sheep, an innovation to keep the newly shorn ewes from freezing during lambing. This novelty was soon dropped because the ewes sometimes lay down and, with their plastic raincoats, could not get up on the slippery grass. Even worse, some ewes failed to seek sheltered spots for lambing if their own bodies were warm from wearing coats; their newborn lambs suffered hypothermia and died.

One of the most enthralling events on the sheep station was shearing, which took place twice a year at Ruby Hills — in February for the wethers (castrated male sheep) and rams, and in August for the ewes. The shearing shed was the heart of the ranch, not just physically but also in terms of activities and lore. Made of galvanized tin walls and a metal roof (when it rained, no one could carry on a conversation), it had a tallowwood floor that was "polished" by many thousands of woolly sheep passing over it. The wool, with its greasy lanolin, gave the wood a special luster and smell. Our shed had seven stands (that is, seven shearers could shear at once), which classified it as a large shed. The building was on stilts, with a large holding area under the main floor for sheep to huddle out of the rain. The sheep were herded up a ramp into each shearing stand, shorn, then pushed down a chute into a holding pen back at ground level. Shearing was obviously a traumatic experience for any sheep, and the shed was chaotic with their bleating, dogs barking, and shearers cursing. A big old hydraulic wool press clanked and creaked loudly as it packed the wool into bales for shipping and selling. Every season, stories circulated about a presser in the district who had mangled his arm in the sharp prongs of the wool press — a disastrous accident.

We never had a female shearer, probably because of the strict regulations of the union. Only occasionally did women even enter the shed during shearing, and they were usually married to shearers. The few who did work were limited to rouseabouts (sweepers) or wool rollers (who pulled the bits of dirty wool off the fleece). The shearers were diverse and colorful, and the influx of these big, strong men into the district each year certainly livened the pastoral scene. Some were regulars, but many were transients from New Zealand or Western Australia.

Shearers pursued a fairly nomadic lifestyle, and their work was extremely rough. If a shearer managed to make enough money at this trade (wages were determined by the number of sheep shorn), often his back would go out or arthritis would develop. If he nicked a sheep and it drew blood, he had to stitch it up himself. Shearers were also known to fall victim to the local pubs after payday. During many shearing seasons we were awakened in the middle of the night to help tow a shearer's car out of a muddy roadside ditch. Despite these drawbacks, it was a romantic vocation, and shearing time always seemed to make the station more spirited and energetic. Even the dogs seemed to run faster, sensing the excitement.

When all the thousands of sheep had been shorn and returned to their paddocks looking like bags of bones, the wool was loaded onto an enormous truck in bales that were sorted by wool type. The wool classer was one of the most important hands during shearing. It was he who determined wool quality and sorted it accordingly. The best and finest wool was Superfine AAA, followed by AA and A, and the least desirable was the skirtings or pieces (the dirty wool or the "daggy" wool picked from around the sheep's buttocks). Wool prices were determined by market demand, as well as by cleanliness and by the thickness of the wool, measured in microns. Because we raised merinos, our wool averaged 19 microns, which is classified as fine wool. In the mid-1980s, this wool was much desired by European clothiers and sold for a relatively high price. In contrast, the dirty, coarser wool such as the skirtings sold for half or even a quarter of the price per bale. Coarse wool was often used for carpets.

Our wool was sold in Newcastle, and I loved to watch the auctions. They were premier social events, attended by all of the graziers in the district, plus their wives and children. If sales were strong and bidders paid high prices, the families would go out and buy new clothes, new kitchen appliances, and perhaps even new furniture for the living room. Usually the women were in charge of spending the wool checks, while the men went to the pub to celebrate. But if prices were down, everyone would commiserate at the pub or at parties held by the wool agents. Because my husband's parents still ran the farm, they managed the checkbook. So I never really felt the emotions of the wool sales in the same way as those who handled the finances. I used to enjoy watching my mother-in-law rush eagerly to an exquisite home-furnishings store, where she bought lovely kitchenware, crystal, and other niceties. Sheep farming was an economic roller-coaster ride—good years followed by bad years and vice versa—and required a certain gambling spirit to endure the fluctuations.

Like the wool market, the dieback problem was emotional. How did you explain to a farmer, who loved his landscape and worried about his trees, that his grazing practices were contributing to their deaths? He needed the livestock to make a living, but he wanted the trees to conserve his soil and provide shade for his stock. It was a difficult task to link land-use practices to dieback, because there was no short-term experiment to make the connection convincing. Instead, long-term observations and innumerable measurements of different aspects of the landscape were needed to understand what was contributing to tree decline.

The study of dieback illustrated the synergistic effects of the various factors. The entire ecosystem required study, not just the livestock or the insects or the foliage of the gum trees. Full comprehension of such a complex system, with its many species and its many changes over time, could not be achieved in a short period. Ecosystems in general are poorly understood owing to a lack of long-term research, and the dieback problem in Australia is only one example. As we continue to alter the natural conditions of our planet, such environmental dilemmas become more commonplace, and the time frames required to solve them exceed the patience of most humans—and the longevity of most scientific grants.

Short-term solutions occasionally were applied, but had little success. In the case of eucalypt dieback, trees could be sprayed with insecticide to kill the Christmas beetles, but this procedure was expensive and localized in its effect. Similarly, most farmers applied superphosphate to enrich their soils (generally via large-scale aerial spraying) but this strategy too was expensive and could have disastrous long-term impacts downstream. More permanent ecological solutions involved the reforestation of patches of land with native trees, interspersed with pasturelands of native grasses. These ecologically based long-term solutions tended to cost a great deal in the short term.

For the first year of my married life, I loved juggling the challenges of scientific research and housewifery. I seem to have treated both as sciences — in one I measured the phenomena of nature, and in one I practiced empirically in the home. I spent two or three days at the university, reading and analyzing data and interacting with colleagues (all male: there were no females as either graduate or postdoctoral students, or as professors in zoology, and very few in other departments). I also used these "town" days for shopping, having mastered the fine art of rapid-shopping for all the necessary foods, tools, and hardware required at home on the land. I also learned to drive home at breakneck speed (avoiding kangaroos by sheer luck, I am embarrassed to admit) along the winding roads, in order to have a hot meal on the table when my grazier husband returned sweaty and tired from the paddock. There were distinct roles in our rural household, and despite my devotion to career, I was determined to successfully personify what was expected of a grazier's wife. I developed a set of menus that were conducive to cooking after a day in town — home-cooked delights that could be created in less than an hour. I altered these quick-cooking days with larger, more extravagant feasts that could be prepared during my "writing days" at home. I tried to be sensitive to balancing home and career, even in a culinary sense. I became adept at "boiling the billy" (making a cup of tea) and learned at least a hundred ways (or so it seemed) to cook lamb. Andrew needed a substantial meal of meat and potatoes and vegetables after a strenuous physical day in the paddocks, and I did not want to shirk my duty to supply it. With the watchful eyes of friends and in-laws on me, I pursued my housewifery with great seriousness, in addition to my science. I secretly believed that if my in-laws could see that scientific pursuits did not preclude attention to housewifery, then they might be supportive of my academic career.

After a year of married life in the bush, however, it became increasingly obvious to me that my devotion to science was an obvious deterrent from domestic duties. A poem (in a diary given to me by my sister-in-law; perhaps she was trying to offer subtle guidance) by Australian Ralph Northwood summarizes the traditional aspirations of women living in the Australian outback.

Country-Women
They're the wives and the mothers of men on the land;
Just cooking, encouraging, lending a hand.
Their homes are in ever such out-of-the-way nooks,
On sun-blistered plains, or beside hidden brooks;
And many harsh trials are the test of their worth —
The floors of their "mansions" are often of earth,
Wetted down with a sluicing of water hard won
From the rim of some dam on a desolate "run."

There's the bread to be baked in a hot oven when
The thermometer stands at a hundred-and-ten.
There are cows to be tended, and calves to be fed,
And sometimes her man needs "a hand in the shed."

Perchance there are babies to bear and to keep,
Where there's no "Dr. Truby" to lull them to sleep;
Where each infant illness is something of "hell"
To the mother, who's nursemaid and doctor as well . . .

You may not be proud of the shack you inhabit,
Perhaps there's no cash, through the drought, plague or rabbit;
But you manage, somehow, to make that shack "HOME."
Your whole selfless life is an unwritten poem
Of sacrifice, love, and a comradely strength,
Inspiring your man to go every length
In his battle with seasons, with "hoppers," and blight —
You make it worth while to go on with the fight!

Like the dieback, my husband and I faced a complex set of factors
that influenced our lives. We had both been raised as part of a generation that promised opportunities for women and encouraged careers for minorities. But Andrew worked for his parents, who represented more conservative values. They truly hoped we would be like
them, filling traditional roles on the farm, because the arrangement
worked so well for them. Could we juggle these two conflicting value
systems, theirs and ours? Or would we succumb to unrest and dis-
satisfaction in our marriage if neither side could convince the other?
I drew many parallels between the frustrations of women living in
rural Australia and the maladies of the trees. Neither situation was
simple, nor was there a clear-cut cause or solution.

Dieback was an ecological illness of great magnitude, enormous
complexity, and a variety of causes. It was not deliberately brought
about by human activity, but in many cases the pattern and intensity
of land use appeared to be the ultimate cause, abetted by secondary
factors such as insects, fungi, and drought. The 1980s saw much
progress on this topic, but no ultimate solutions. Our work on
dieback did not have a happy ending, and remains open-ended.

More funds are desperately needed. Who should pay for trees — the landowners who raise the sheep and indirectly contribute to degradation of the landscape, or the government who taxes the landowners, who then need to rear more livestock in order to make a living? What about the tourists and city folks who want to see healthy gum trees on a picturesque pastoral landscape, instead of withered and dying gray skeletons? Each of us has a share of blame for having neglected and abused the environment and ignored signs of its deterioration. Scientists, graziers, farmers, economists, foresters, land managers, politicians, and taxpayers together share the responsibility for finding a cure for dieback, for preventing its further occurrence, and for regenerating a dying landscape.

3 Canopies near the Ground

*T*his is the great age, make no mistake about it; the robot has been born somewhat appropriately along with the atom bomb, and the brain they say now is just another type of more complicated feedback system. The engineers have its basic principles worked out; it's mechanical, you know; nothing to get superstitious about; and man can always improve on nature once he gets the idea. Well, he's got it all right and that's why, I guess, that I sit here in my chair . . . remembering those two birds and blue mountain sunlight. There is another article on my desk that reads "Machines Are Getting Smarter Every Day." I don't deny it, but I'll stick with the birds. It's life I believe in, not machines. —Loren Eisley, *The Immense Journey,* 1946

In a forest, insects are like tiny grains of sand — almost impossible to see, to count, or to observe individually. How does one follow the journey of a caterpillar through the complex maze of branches and foliage in a tall tree? And what happens to a larva that falls off a leaf when a bird alights and displaces it? These and other hypotheses cannot be addressed in a complex rain forest. To answer questions that were impossible to ask in tall treetops, I visited a simple canopy system closer to the ground: the low-lying vegetation on coral islands. During my years as a graduate and postdoctoral student, I had the good fortune to participate in research projects on coral reef islands, called cays. I assisted fellow graduate students with their reef research, and in exchange they accompanied me on rain-forest climbing expeditions.

The Great Barrier Reef in Australia extends 1,600 kilometers from the Torres Straits to the Bunker Islands, along the coast of the state of Queensland. Reefs and islands are scattered throughout 200,000 square kilometers of the Coral Sea. The coral islands, also called cays, contain isolated patches of vegetation that are simple both structurally and floristically. For example, One Tree Island (23°30' south latitude, 152°8' east longitude) has only 21 permanent plant species. These include 128 individual bushes of Argusia argentea, *a prostrate, continuous-leafing shrub whose distribution extends throughout the Indo-Pacific from East Africa to the East Indies.* Argusia *is the host plant to a monophagous larva of the moth* Utetheisa pulchelloides *(family Arctiidae). The caterpillars are abundant and hatch throughout the year. In addition,* Argusia *is found on many of the outlying coral islands, providing wonderfully isolated natural laboratories for unorthodox pursuits such as caterpillar watching!*

Every wage-earner has a retirement plan. As a canopy biologist, my retirement plan is seedlings and shrubs. By cultivating an interest in plants close to the ground, I will have a secondary focus when I am too old to climb trees.

As the ship left Gladstone Harbor, the air was still and ominous. Eerie dark clouds hung low, pierced by golden lines from the setting sun. Screaming gulls broke the menacing silence. We stood on the deck, hushed and spellbound, wondering how safe it was to set sail directly into the eye of a cyclone. Captain Max assured us that the eye was moving eastward more rapidly than the ship. As long as the storm did not change direction, we should be able to remain on our schedule of visiting eight reefs and surveying six uninhabited coral islands during a ten-day period.

The offshore winds generated some rough seas, and I spent a claustrophobic night in my upper berth just beneath the ship's bow. A greasy chicken dinner, supplemented by the smell of old sneakers strewn on the cabin floor, brought on my first-ever bout of seasickness. Most of my scientist colleagues struggled too with the combination of a heavy meal and rough seas. The distant sounds of retching in the latrines scarcely eased my own delicate condition.

Our boat, the *Australiana,* accommodated fifteen of us. Scientists and assistants, we were a varied lot: ornithologists, algologists, geologists, herpetologists, marine biologists, and plant ecologists. Our mission was to document the flora and fauna of the Swain Reefs, the southeasternmost chain of the Great Barrier Reef islands. The islands of Swain Reefs were not populated by humans, although one boasted the remnants of a primitive camp and another had a rudimentary weather tower. Relatively young in geological time, the cays were in various stages of colonization, ranging from no resident vegetation to as many as eleven species of plants. The animal population exploded seasonally during the months of seabird nesting, which contributed nutrients to the developing soils from guano and bio-

The coral cays in the Swain Reefs section of the Great Barrier Reef, offshore from southeastern Queensland. This is prime territory for sea snakes, and the route of our boat trip to survey them is shown. Illustration by Barbara Harrison.

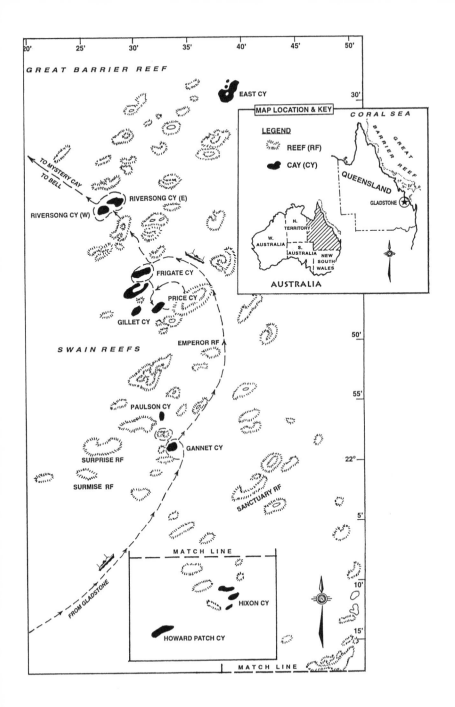

mass from chick mortality. The birds were also a principal source of seed dispersal for most of the coral cay plants. Once the plants had arrived, the insects that ate them usually became established as well.

Our expedition leader, Professor Harold (Hal) Heatwole, had been surveying populations of sea snakes in the waters of the Swain Reefs for more than fifteen years. He and his faithful graduate students devoted their energies to locating, retrieving, handling, and marking the snakes via a painless freeze-dried branding technique. Every year they returned to reweigh and remeasure the population. Using this mark-and-recapture technique, they learned that sea snakes had very well defined territories or home ranges. In fact, one sea snake may spend its entire lifespan of ten years or more on a single patch reef!

Like canopy research, marine biology has suffered from the absence of viable methods to document the biology of organisms, in this case those that live underwater. The development of scuba diving in the 1950s resulted in a substantial expansion of our knowledge of marine fish, corals, and sea snakes. (Similarly, the development of single-rope technique and canopy walkways in the 1980s created an explosion of studies in tree crowns that is often compared to the advent of scuba.) Now that diving is commonplace, biologists have been able to count, observe, and monitor sea snakes and their environment.

Snakes are reputed to be the most recently evolved group of reptiles, originating from lizards in the late Jurassic period (over 130 million years ago). The family Elapidae includes terrestrial, venomous snakes with hollow fangs. In this group also are the present-day marine snakes which are so recent in evolution that no fossils exist. Of fifteen extant families of snakes, four have marine species that include forty-seven species of true sea snakes. Water temperature is a limiting factor in sea-snake distribution, and these creatures occur only in warm tropical and subtropical oceans. As reptiles, snakes have two chief modes of reproduction. Some are oviparous and lay eggs; others are vivaparous and give birth to live young. Our study snake, the olive sea snake *(Aipysurus laevis,* family Hydrophiidae), is vivaparous and also venomous.

Sea snakes have different adaptations from their land cousins. They must be able to get rid of excess salt, and obtain fresh water and oxygen for bodily functions. They require different modes of propulsion in water than on land, and different sensory mechanisms to obtain food, find mates, and establish territory. Sea snakes feed by moving slowly along the bottom, extending their tongues against corals and into crevices to detect prey via smell. Their vision is very poor, and occasionally they capture prey by bumping into it. Their venom is poisonous enough to kill scores of laboratory mice in a single dose. Why so toxic? Perhaps so that their prey die immediately when they are bitten, instead of swimming out of sight.

My ship duties—thank goodness—were of a terrestrial nature. I had come along to map and survey the vegetation, as well as to conduct some ecological experiments on low-lying island shrubs. During our days at sea, I assisted with the sea-snake research. I confess that I was not enthusiastic about swimming among representatives of this venomous species. Despite the fact that the sea snake has poor vision and is fairly docile in most natural situations, a mistaken swish of the flipper could exact revenge on even the most unsuspecting snorkeler. One bite from a sea snake can be fatal. Its venom is much more toxic than that of the eastern diamondback rattlesnake. There is an antidote, but it is not frequently administered because of the risk of anaphylactic shock. Relatively few medical books offer suggestions on how to deal with a sea-snake bite—especially hundreds of kilometers offshore from the nearest hospital.

To capture sea snakes for measurement, our brave team swam slowly and gingerly through different patch reefs. Their butterfly nets adeptly swept the gently swimming serpents into temporary captivity. The snakes were then transferred into garbage bins on one of our dinghies, where they quickly became an angry, writhing mass of toxic fury, unhappily displaced from their aqueous medium. The garbage bins from each dinghy were brought to the deck of the ship every few hours, where Hal delicately plucked out each snake, measured it, recorded its number (which looked like a tattoo along its abdomen), and returned it to the water. Unmarked snakes were freeze-branded with a new number and added to the population census.

On January 20, I loyally volunteered to take my turn at sea-snake capture. I was not a parent then, or I probably would never have made such a daring offer. We were at the patch reefs adjacent to Mystery Cay; even the name conjured up adventure. Armed with a net and my snorkeling gear, I slipped into the water. As I gazed anxiously around the reef, chaetadons (butterfly fish) swam by, their beautiful yellow-and-black patterns reflecting the sun like jewels. The corals, diverse and magnificent, ranged from the spindles of the staghorn corals to the large, spherical brain corals. The reef was truly a spectacular site, but I did not appreciate it that day. I was on a mission, and my eyes were searching exclusively for the image of a snake. Some patch reefs have abundant sea-snake populations and some have none. Herpetologists are still trying to determine the reason: is it food supply? predators? reef size?

As luck would have it, I immediately spotted a thin, brown apparition swimming lazily toward me. Even without my glasses, I could hardly fail to recognize what it was. The sea snake did not seem vicious; nonetheless, the concept of this poison machine coming within striking range was difficult to accept calmly. But the safest behavior was to remain still. I froze. The snake swam up close and "kissed" my face mask. It was torture to remain absolutely station-

One of the most frightening moments of my life: coming face to face with
an olive sea snake, one of the world's most poisonous creatures.
Illustration by Barbara Harrison.

ary while the snake sniffed my face and neck. I closed my eyes tightly,
unable to watch. When I opened them several seconds later, the
snake was gone — vanished. Not only had I shown extraordinary fear,
but I had also failed to capture my prey. When I got back on the ship,
my colleagues laughed uproariously. How could anyone who
climbed tall trees be frightened of a small brown snake? I could not
answer that question, but I was relieved to be relegated to steno-
graphic duties on the safety of the deck.

Hal handled and measured the snakes; I recorded the data. We
were a fine team and I enjoyed my post aboard ship. Our peaceful
procedure was abruptly halted as Hal was tossing snake #470 back
into a patch of ocean called Isobel Reef. Within a millisecond, it

turned and bit him on the finger. In several decades of snake handling, Hal had almost never been bitten and definitely not by *Aipysurus laevis,* the queen mother of all poisonous snakes.

Reacting in true scientific spirit, Hal calmly handed me his camera and notebook, and requested that I chronicle the progress of his symptoms, should they prove to be serious. Because no one had ever fully documented the death syndrome caused by this species of sea snake, he was determined that his mistake at least be recorded. I nervously snapped a few photos, then we proceeded to measure the remaining sea snakes in the garbage bin.

By this time, Captain Max was aware of the commotion on deck. Everyone who had returned from snorkeling heard about Hal's mishap, and many were anxiously photographing his ill-fated finger. Max became agitated: no captain wants a dead body on shipboard, regardless of the cause. Captain Max called the flying doctor service and requested that a seaplane be dispatched immediately to take Hal to a hospital on the mainland. In almost no time, a plane was heard in the distance. Max threw a flare that lit up the sky. The tiny seaplane landed alongside the boat, and Hal was transferred into it. Needless to say, our crew had lost its enthusiasm for research. We sat quietly for the rest of the day, sharing Hal's lifetime accomplishments and virtues. It was a dismal time for all. Our spirited leader was in danger of dying, a victim of his own research subject. After a quiet dinner we went to bed early.

At dawn I woke to the jubilant cheers of Captain Max and rushed on deck to hear the news. To everyone's relief, Hal had not only survived the night in the hospital, but was returning to the ship the next day. Some snakebites cause a physical wound but do not result in the injection of venom. This apparently was one of those cases. (In later years, a photograph of Hal's bite was published in a snake textbook; fortunately, that was the only legacy of his misadventure.) We sailed off into the rising sun to proceed with our infinitely more benign terrestrial work on the coral islands.

The coral cays of the Swain Reefs had wonderful names — Riversong East, Riversong West, Mystery Cay, Bell Cay, Frigate Cay, Gillett Cay, Price Cay, Gannet Cay, and even the newly formed Howard Patch, where five of us stood on this tiny island that occupied only 6 square meters. Our expedition had the privilage of naming this new island, but ten years later, I cannot remember who Howard was. On the younger cays the vegetation was barely established and we worked hard to locate any resident plants. On older cays, such as Bell or Frigate, the land was obviously more established and plant diversity ranged up to eleven species.

I used the low-lying *Argusia* shrubs to explore several questions about caterpillar behavior that were difficult to investigate in a three-dimensional forest ecosystem:

1. What were the feeding rates of the moth larvae on their food plant?
2. Could these herbivores navigate back to their host bush if disturbed from a branch?
3. Did herbivores have a negative effect on the growth and survival of coral island vegetation?

Argusia grew on open beaches, usually just above the high-tide line, although sometimes extending into the interior. This tendency to grow on exposed island edges was probably a consequence of its seed dispersal via ocean currents. In fact, saltwater exposure appeared to be a prerequisite to germination (as opposed to most plants, whose seeds die if exposed to salt water). The critical factors affecting the survival of *Argusia* shrubs were the physical environment (salt and wind exposure) and the availability of fresh water and nutrients. The prostrate growth form of *Argusia* created an almost

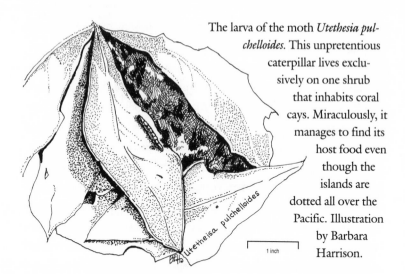

The larva of the moth *Utethesia pulchelloides*. This unpretentious caterpillar lives exclusively on one shrub that inhabits coral cays. Miraculously, it manages to find its host food even though the islands are dotted all over the Pacific. Illustration by Barbara Harrison.

two-dimensional system, conducive to behavioral studies of caterpillars on their host plant. *Utethesia pulchelloids* (family Aretiidae) was a moth whose catepillars fed exclusively on *Argusia* shrubs.

I experimentally removed caterpillars from shrubs to see whether or not they could navigate back to their home bush. Thirty caterpillars were marked in the field with drops of colored nail polish on their dorsal sides. They were observed at hourly intervals for their movement, feeding, or resting activities. Ten were tracked for up to nineteen days. Their home range, distance traveled, and number of leaves visited were all calculated. I found that caterpillars during the day allocated 53 percent of their time to feeding, 8 percent to traveling, and 39 percent to resting. Compared to human schedules, the time allocated for eating seemed disproportionate, but in nature many vegetarians need to feed more continuously than carnivores. Over a ten-day period (their lifespan) larvae traveled an average of 17 feet, but sometimes remained on one leaf throughout an entire day. When a caterpillar moved, it often crossed several leaves before stopping to feed. It never fed from a leaf that was already partially chewed. Scientists have found that leaves with holes inflicted by other herbivores may sequester toxins in the partially eaten leaf, a process that serves to protect the leaves from further damage. Thus, insects are well advised to avoid leaves with holes, in order to minimize their consumption of toxins.

The larvae ate different amounts of foliage on different islands. For example, on Bell Cay the shrubs lost approximately 18 percent of their leaf area to herbivores, whereas on One Tree Island only 2 percent was eaten. The number of caterpillars and the number of bushes were different on each island. Presumably, as the insect populations grew, leaf consumption would increase. In classic insect outbreaks, the number of insects eventually exceeds the available food supply, and plants suffer complete defoliation or even mortality. Insects also suffer mortality if their food supply becomes locally extinct, or if a predator or parasite preys on them. There are many unknowns regarding the colonization of populations on cays, islands, or other isolated ecosystems. For example, are there minimum and maximum critical populations? How do plants and insects disperse onto isolated islands? If they become extinct, will they recolonize in the future? All of these questions have become increasingly meaningful for conservation of various fragmented ecosystems that represent "islands" surrounded by developed landscapes.

During my graduate-student years, I spent time in residence on both Heron and One Tree islands, usually as a field assistant to fellow students who were studying marine ecology. Not only did I learn about coral reef fish biology and diversity of corals, but I also experienced life as a graduate student at a marine field station. One of my most vivid recollections is the challenge of sleeping at Heron Island, the marine research station for the University of Queensland. Like many coral cays, Heron had a seasonal population of wedge-tailed shearwaters. These birds roosted at night in sandy burrows under and adjacent to our cabins. Their communication and courtship involved continuous loud moaning, which began with low chortling sounds and built to a raucous crescendo. It was impossible to sleep through this scenario and, worse, the adult birds often bumped into the cabin walls or even slid through doors left ajar, as they awkwardly tried to land near their burrows and locate their families. Like many seabirds, shearwaters could not take off or land with much agility; they needed a runway.

The emotional lives of marine graduate students always seemed much more colorful than those of my terrestrial comrades. Maybe it was the notion of being on an island paradise, or maybe it was simply the late-night hours that everyone kept in light of the bird noises. Maybe it was because everyone took the nocturnal exploits of the birds to be the sexual exploits of graduate students! Whatever the case, when I visited Heron or One Tree islands I always felt as if I had been on the set of an afternoon soap opera. The stories collected there may in themselves constitute a future book.

Because of my extended visits to One Tree Island, I was able to count the number of bushes there and calculate the exact impact of caterpillars on the plant community. (And yes, there really was only one tree, or rather one small clump of *Pisonia* palms, in the center of the island.) An average caterpillar consumed 2.9 square centimeters of leaf area during its ten days of existence. One hundred twenty-eight bushes had 227,082 leaves (equal to 1,146 square centimers of leaf area or 160.9 kilograms of dry weight). Since 2 percent of the leaf surface was removed, it represented 21 square meters or 3 kilograms of leaf material, a relatively insignificant amount in terms of the overall health of these shrubs. In other studies scientists have shown that moderate levels of herbivory can actually stimulate plant growth, much the way mowing the lawn stimulates the growth of grass.

To test the ability of caterpillars to navigate in a complex "sea of green," I experimentally dislodged them from their home branch and placed them at intervals around the base of a bush. They required an average of thirty minutes — and traveled randomly up to 30 meters — to relocate their home bush, which was only two minutes (and 2 meters) away. This poor ability to navigate suggests that if a caterpillar is dislodged from its host plant in a complex forest, it most likely will die.

In my second study of island vegetation, I looked at the diversity and regeneration of plants on coral cays. I placed yellow stakes at 1-meter intervals through the center of each cay and experimentally removed a swath of vegetation. I sampled six cays, ranging from youthful (with one plant species) to relatively old (up to eight plant

Conducting botanical surveys on coral reef islands. As a canopy researcher experienced in tall trees, I took great joy in the low-lying canopies (or lack thereof), which facilitated simpler experiments and different types of data collection. Black-faced boobies were my companions in setting up transects and measuring the colonization of vegetation and subsequent insect herbivory on these islands. Photograph by David Lowman.

species present). Every winter and summer I recorded what was re-generating and measured the density of regrowth.

This study came to an unfortunate end after three years, when I discovered an artifact of sampling. In field biology, scientists work very hard to design experiments and to take measurements on systems that have no artificial impacts. Frequently this was not easy to do and sometimes biased results occurred. In this instance, my yellow stakes created convenient roosting sites for seabirds. While I did not mind their use of my transect, I did mind the significant influx of bird guano onto my experimental squares, for the extra nutrients may have provided an unfair advantage to some or all of the regenerating plants. In short, my measurements were biased. I was forced to abandon the study until I could design a stake that would not allow birds to roost.

The challenges of carrying out field experiments under rigorous conditions are enormous, but the challenges of setting up valid experiments — and of recognizing factors that may bias the results — are perhaps the greatest responsibility of scientists. The possibilities of improperly sampling both simple shrubs and complex tall trees, are equally strong. But the dangers involved in research in tree canopies make it compelling to attempt to design experiments carefully so that such difficult field work will not be undertaken in vain.

Another serious challenge facing scientists who work in undisturbed ecosystems is the moral obligation to keep the systems in their natural state. Islands are very delicate ecosystems; their small size and isolation from the mainland often magnify the impact of extinction and the introduction of exotics. The invasion of a pest can wreak havoc on the local vegetation. Similarly, the damage caused by human litter or clearing can be equally destructive to the natural equilibrium, or balance of nature. Hal Heatwole describes the precautions he took during the early expeditions of marine biologists to One Tree, before the island was inhabited:

> A covered plastic rubbish bin containing sea water covered with a layer of motor oil several centimeters thick was used as a receptacle for all food scraps and empty food tins. A second such container served as a latrine. These containers were removed from the island following each trip. . . . Only tinned food was consumed while on the island and hence fresh food was not available to serve as a nutrient source for local insects. Leftovers were not kept for later meals but were discarded in the bin with motor oil. After meals utensils and dishes were washed in sea water which was then discarded in the bin. . . . A gas lamp was used one evening outside the tent and attracted a number of. . . . moths, five of which flew into the lamp and were killed. . . . Subsequently we used flashlights outside and when a gas lamp was used inside the tent, the zippers of the tent were secured, making it insectproof. When persons entered or left when the light was on, the zipper was opened as briefly as possible and only far enough to allow the person to pass. (H. Heatwole, T. Done, and E. Cameron, "Community Ecology of a Coral Cay, A Study of One Tree Island, Great Barrier Reef," 1981)

I spent my first Christmas away from family in 1979 on One Tree Island. Four of us who were scientists lived in a simple tin-roofed shed. For our Christmas tree, we collected a dead branch from an *Argusia* shrub and hung bits of bleached dead coral on it. There were no telephones to call home, no packages or mail. We managed to sing a few sorrowful carols under the hot sun and take a Christmas snorkel. I had the double loneliness of "celebrating" my birthday two days prior to Christmas. Two graduate students kindly cooked a birthday feast that consisted of bivalve soup, coral trout, and (warm) gin and tonic.

Food was imported to One Tree Island in boxes packed by the grocery store on the mainland. It was challenging to plan a menu for two to three weeks. For example, milk — if brought frozen in cartons — would last approximately a week as it gradually thawed in the island kitchen. Canned food was the most reliable staple. We counted on the *Siganid* fish to recycle our waste material. (Everyone who has worked on One Tree Island is familiar with the region of beach affectionately called the gutter — not the spot for leisurely snorkeling.) One Tree Island had outbreaks of ants and cockroaches, and the population of gulls doubled because of the human presence. Silver eyes came into the kitchen hut and observed how to tip over the sugar container — not a behavior that had been useful for past generations of those birds. Overall, the vegetation and the reefs were relatively undisturbed. There were important trade-offs between allowing scientists to work at a minimal level of survivability with their tools of the trade and at the same time being responsible stewards of an ecosystem.

What did my studies in low-lying canopies teach me? For caterpillars, remaining on or near their food plant is imperative. In forests, beetle larvae sometimes rain out of tree canopies when birds alight or when winds disturb the foliage. These events undoubtedly lead to mortality of thousands of larvae who cannot navigate back up into the canopy of their host plant. Caterpillars are generally sedentary, and an accidental fall is probably fatal. In both forests and coral islands, insect herbivores prefer shade leaves to sun leaves. Several explanations are possible. The leaves in the shade may be softer, or lower in compounds that are toxic to the herbivores, or more nutritious; or perhaps the chance of being eaten by predators is higher in the sun leaves; or perhaps the challenge of feeding in sunny conditions is more stressful than in shade owing to desiccation, salt, and wind exposure. It is likely that all these factors collectively contribute to the behavior of caterpillars. Even in a relatively simple situation (low-lying shrubs on an isolated coral island), the interactions between insects and plants are extraordinarily complicated. Scientists must become detectives to unmask the clues and unravel the mysteries of the complex machinery we call an ecosystem.

4 Research and Motherhood

*T*here are some who can live with wild things and
some who cannot. Like winds and sunsets, wild
things were taken for granted until progress began
to do away with them. Now we face the question whether a
still higher "standard of living" is worth its cost in things
natural, wild, and free. For us of the minority, the opportunity to see geese is more important than television, and the
chance to find a pasque-flower is a right as inalienable as
free speech.

—Aldo Leopold, *A Sand County Almanac,* 1949

In the midst of contemplating the mysteries of life and death in forests, my own biological clock was ticking away. When my first son Edward was born in 1985, I was forced to take on the delicate science of juggling. Passionate about my career, yet fully committed to parenthood and housewifery, I could never have been adequately prepared for the challenges involved. I still wonder if a female mentor in my biological career would have helped me make better decisions, or at least be wiser about what lay ahead. But, I knew of no women scientists in Australia who during the 1970s and 1980s were botany professors.

In 1984 I became pregnant, a condition the Australians call having a bun in the oven. This occurrence perhaps alleviated some of the anxiety about my career that I sensed from my inlaws. I worried that my reproductive abilities were appreciated far more than my scientific mind. Were their apparent priorities a harbinger of things to come, or was I merely experiencing an emotional surge of my hormones during pregnancy?

My first suspicions of pregnancy arose while I was perched in the canopy of a black bean tree *(Castonospermum australis,* family Fabaceae) in north Queensland. I had flown up to Atherton, headquarters of the CSIRO Rain Forest Research Unit. I was assisting one of the scientific staff in setting up a phenology study that used a tower in the midst of a black-bean stand. Under normal conditions, canopy work from a stable tower was a virtual joy for me, compared to working from swaying ropes. But this time I became very dizzy and nauseous. My body felt different. These symptoms made me so skeptical that I sneaked out to the corner store that evening and bought a paperback on pregnancy, the only book on the topic in the store. With only male scientists other than myself on this expedition, I had no one to ask about my symptoms. In the safety of my bedcovers, I read the book by flashlight. All of the descriptions seemed to match my condition, but I had to wait until my return to Walcha to confirm my suspicions. Accompanying me on this research trip to Queensland was an undergraduate student from the University of Minnesota whom I was mentoring, so I confided my thoughts to her. To this day, we share the humor of having whispered in the Australian bush about my first pregnancy. (I was thrilled to get news in 1994 of the arrival of her own first child.) I am delighted that — ten years later — she had women mentors in graduate school with whom to share these issues.

Two weeks later, back at my doctor's office in Walcha, I tested positive. My suspicions about the subtle changes in my body had been correct. Although ultrasounds were not available here in the outback, I was confident that the baby was a boy. I gained almost fifty pounds, and my tiny stature mushroomed. The baby thrashed and kicked constantly during my last trimester, so I truly looked forward to the delivery of our large progeny. Throughout the nine months I continued my fieldwork, albeit with some modification. Instead of using ropes and harness, I allowed myself the luxury of a cherry picker for access to tree canopies. My field assistant, Wayne Higgins, was a true gentleman. He drove the bucket very gently, accommodating my frequent requests to descend to ground level to relieve my bladder. During the last two months we barely managed to squeeze into the bucket of the cherry picker together — I in the final stages of pregnancy and Wayne with a waistline that testified to his many beers at the local pub. Those nine months also provided a reduced level of physical activity that was conducive to increased writing. By acknowledging the limitations of my body, I hoped that motherhood could be compatible with a research career.

As with most first pregnancies, the baby was late. I went to the hospital prematurely, having experienced sharp pangs of false labor for twenty-four hours. Returning home, at the suggestion of my mother-in-law I ate Chinese food and then walked extensively over

The cherry picker, another useful tool for canopy access. I found it especially helpful when I was pregnant; my swollen tummy would have ruled out single ropes with their harness apparatus. I used the cherry picker in dry eucalypt stands to study the widespread forest dieback in Australia. Illustration by Barbara Harrison.

the rough furrows in the back pasture. The next morning (after seeing more than a hundred black-necked storks — also called jabirus — in our back yard!) I was admitted at 11:00 A.M. I was in labor all day and into the evening. The baby was in a breech position and simply did not want to move. I was exhausted, but no pain medication or drugs were available in this rural hospital. I had faith in my physician, who advised me that he would call the flying doctor service to transport me to a city hospital if complications arose.

At midnight the labor table in the delivery room collapsed while I was still on it. Fortunately, Andrew had a toolbox in his truck and made temporary repairs. At approximately 1:00 A.M. the doctor, recognizing my state of exhaustion, told me to cut loose with a string of curse words to ease my stress. Perhaps because of my lack of energy, all I could manage was "Jeepers creepers." There are not many swear words in my normal vocabulary, and I was not about to develop them in this exhausted state. (The story of my childbirth "cursing" made me a local laughingstock for many months afterward!) I can hardly remember anything, but Edward Arthur Burgess was born at 1:22 A.M. He weighed 8½ pounds. After thirty-six long hours of labor without pain killers, I promptly fell asleep. The doctor performed what he called quilting on my underpinnings, to repair the tears that resulted from delivering such a large baby. But all was well, and since no other babies were born in the hospital that week, I had the luxury of a seven-day hospital recovery.

Our first son was named after his maternal great-grandfather and my brother (both Edward), and his paternal great-grandfather (Arthur Burgess). I was extremely fond of all three men. My own grandfather had been a kind, wonderful friend to my two brothers and me as children. My husband's grandfather, Arthur, was probably my closest friend on the farm. We shared a love of nature and delighted in exchanging conversation about birds observed, flowers noted, or simply the change of seasons. I often invited him to afternoon tea or to dinner, and without voicing criticism, he seemed to enjoy my pursuits of natural history on the eucalypts. Ironically, his level of interest seemed more progressive than that of his son or grandson, but perhaps it was merely that we shared a mutual love of trees. He told me stories about the changes in the landscape at Ruby Hills and recalled amazing details from his childhood when he first walked from Sydney to Walcha as a youth and settled in that district.

He died shortly after Eddie's birth. I secretly believe that he had simply been waiting for the birth of a male heir. I not only lost a loyal friend and relative, but I also lost someone who encouraged my love of the Australian bush. He willed his homestead to Andrew and me, and hardly a day went by that I did not feel his kind spirit within those walls.

Our second son, James Brian Lowman Burgess, arrived in 1987 after a labor of only twelve hours. This time, my practical farming husband (who participated in birthing events on the farm with great frequency) elected to sleep instead of pace the floor with me during my nocturnal hours of labor. His reasoning was terribly pragmatic but hardly endearing to a wife. Again I chalked it up to cultural differences. (American couples seem to relish sharing the pregnancy experience: Lamaze classes, books on how to share parenting. In contrast, my Australian pregnancies were solitary experiences.) James was named for the first Burgess who traveled from Scotland to Australia to settle over one hundred years ago, and also for his paternal grandfather, Brian. I loved and respected my father-in-law for his excellence and passion in farm management; his wisdom regarding sheep and cattle was unsurpassed throughout the district.

The birth of two sons who represented the fifth generation on a large rural Australian station seemed to signify an end to my career aspirations. It was not exactly the philosophy I had envisioned, but I perceived that parenting was definitely the most acceptable role for me in this setting.

Life at home with two very young children was like no other experience in my entire life. Everything was all so new, and a Ph.D. was totally useless in trying to figure out what makes a baby cry. All four of us were exhausted, and only their father was able to stay relatively sane owing to a schedule that took him out of the house from dawn until dusk. I guess that even the sheep seemed more gratifying than crying children! It was only after Eddie and later James were seven months old and began to eat solid food that they quieted down and actually slept for any duration. My theory—in hindsight—is that each of these big babies had been ready for a steak on his second day, but I simply hadn't figured that out.

My faithful mother traveled 10,000 miles, all the way from New York, to assist me with my first few weeks of mothering, and did so again when James was born. Despite her jet lag, she walked and rocked the baby and allowed me to rest. One day she was walking Eddie down our long dirt driveway when a calico-brown, menacing snake slithered just in front of the carriage. Horrorstruck, she abruptly turned and made a beeline for the house. My father-in-law came along in his four-wheel-drive truck and inquired about her haste. When she described the snake, he chuckled and cheerfully advised her, "One bite and you'd have been dead in ninety seconds." It was a tiger snake, extremely deadly and sometimes aggressive. My mother's respect for my choice of environment to raise children was shattered forever.

Once Eddie had enough food, he was a perfect baby. He loved to play, he slept and ate well, and he quickly learned to communicate. He was my constant companion, even as a toddler trekking out to the forest to check the litter traps, counting beetles on the peppermint saplings, and journeying up to the university for short periods in my office. He was walking and talking in less than a year. I often wonder if he was precocious because he had his mother's constant attention. In a rural situation, there were no distractions. The phone did not ring often; all the members of my immediate family were half a world away; there was no cable television; and there were no day-care options. I gave up the idea of attending conferences or presenting talks because there was no one to mind the baby. I scrambled to write scientific papers during naptime, but my research usually took a distant second place to household chores.

Missing the intellectual company of the university I took up gardening as a poor substitute. I gardened with a passion, determined to create a New England shade garden in honor of my heritage, (and because I lived in the New England district of Australia, where English plants could be grown). I bought rhododendron, Dutchman's breeches, anemone, hellebores, columbine, azalea, and many others. I hoed and dug and scraped and dragged and fertilized and watered—and got very strong. In one section where I had cleared out the rubble, a delicate ancestral rose came up, evidently one that the great-great-grandparents had brought over from the Burgess family home in Scotland. The children's great-grandmother, who had gardened here before me, had also planted many shrubs typical of New England under the treasured shade of the old elms.

Eddie was my gardening assistant. He did a wonderful job of eating dirt and getting it all over his body. He liked to drag the hoses around the flower beds and turn the spigots on or off. I never became comfortable enough to relax when my children were crawling around the garden, for I was uneasily aware of all the poisonous snakes slithering in close proximity. Approximately 95 percent of Australia's snakes are venomous, and for many there was no known antidote to their poison. It was not a comforting thought. My anxieties were confirmed when a brown snake made her nest in our outhouse one spring. We cleared out all her babies, or so we hoped; yet we continued to see brown snakes and black snakes in the garden in great numbers during Eddie's first summer.

One hot day, by chance I had put Eddie in for his nap *before* shifting the hoses. Even though he enjoyed moving them, it had been unusually hot and he was ready to sleep. I went alone into the garden to turn off the tap. As I reached for the nozzle, which stood upright on a pipe in the middle of the flower bed, I was vaguely aware that its location had moved 2 feet from its original position. I came out of my daydream just in time to realize that I was about to close my fist around the head of a brown snake, standing erect in an aggressive stance adjacent to the garden pipe. Quickly running back into the house and locking the door behind me, I breathed a sigh of relief that Eddie had not been on his usual mission to turn off the tap. Any good Australian wife was taught to kill poisonous snakes in the garden, so I loaded up the shotgun and cautiously crept back to the site where the marauder had fooled me. Alas, the snake had disappeared. I was secretly relieved because I was not comfortable using the gun. Needless to say, we did not play in the garden for several days afterward. My Australian husband laughed at my anxiety and suggested that I get used to such a commonplace event.

Most of my young and newly married female friends on neighboring properties had aspirations quite different from those of the previous generation of rural Australian women. They wanted careers and academic degrees that facilitated independence from the farm economy. But it was difficult in the rural sector to pursue such goals, as there were no large population centers that offered job opportunities, cultural outlets or continuing education. In short, despite all the advances of the twentieth century, many of my female friends were frustrated and reconciled to the notion that their lives would be similar to those of their mothers and mothers-in-law. A few found success in endeavors such as running a dress shop, teaching in the district school, or opening a bed-and-breakfast.

I took the last choice, eager to develop a professional outlet for my domestic life. I opened a bed-and-breakfast on our farm, with deluxe accommodations for a couple in a lovely wing adjacent to the house, and basic accommodations for up to four families in the shearing cabins next to the woolshed. I felt a strong urge to have my own earnings, however small, to provide such luxuries as children's books without jeopardizing our normal household expenses — and this operation seemed compatible with housewifery. My new vocation forced me to be organized. I served breakfast on a tray with silver service at 7:30 A.M. (the boys were still babies, so I prayed they would not be screaming), picnic lunch, and then candlelight dinner at 7:00 P.M. (more prayers — I always put the boys to bed early and hoped they would remain there quietly).

Despite the rigors of waiting on guests with young children underfoot, I found the bed-and-breakfast wonderful in two respects. First, it forced me to study the science of organization and apply it to my household. Working out menus, pantry supplies, childrens' versus adults' schedules for eating and washing up all ensured a smooth operation. (This practice really helped me several years later when I became a single parent and had to cope as head of household.) Second, since most of the guests were Americans interested in nature (otherwise they would not have chosen to visit our remote site), I made some congenial friends. In most cases they were extremely surprised to find an expatriate hostess. That provided a fine business advantage because visitors appreciated brewed coffee (rather than the instant served in most homes in Australia), a washcloth in the bathroom (not customary for Australians), and translations of Aussie slang.

The guests loved to see the koalas, kangaroos and other wildlife around the farm. So I devised a self-guided nature trail with pamphlet, which allowed them to see some of the fascinating plants at their leisure. In exchange for their bush experience, the guests provided wonderful insights and moral support, and brought me up to date on American ways. For example, they asked how I managed in such isolation, or how I survived living nextdoor to my in-laws. Only Americans seemed curious enough and brave enough to ask such personal questions (which is why Australians sometimes refer to them as "stickybeaks," a fairly derogatory term for their inquisitiveness). Despite such candid curiosity, I appreciated their interest and empathy.

As I struggled to juggle housewifery, motherhood, and a smattering of science, the dieback situation gained national attention. Hal (my postdoctoral supervisor) and I were asked by a publisher to write a book about it. I was not convinced that I could accomplish such a feat along with my household responsibilities, but Hal — with his prior experience writing books — felt confident that as a team we could succeed. It was a very positive experience for me, because I was able to write much of my portion at home and visit the university library at intervals. We each wrote four chapters, and the entire process was sheer delight. I am grateful to Hal for sharing his expertise with me and for remaining flexible with regard to my domestic tasks. I shall never forget the arrival of our proofs. I was just home from the hospital with James, my second son, and gasped in horror at the thought of getting myself to the university to review the pages. But Hal cheerfully drove to the house and read them to me while I nursed the baby. We actually had fun, and we managed to correct the proofs in timely fashion.

The publisher, recognizing that I lived in the heart of dieback country on a full-fledged rural property, suggested that we organize the book launch in our shearers' shed. It was a gala event, complete with all our neighbors plus many members of the Sydney book world. My husband's family were very cooperative throughout the publication, newspaper interviews and follow-up research activities, but I imagine they fervently hoped that I would soon tire of such academic pursuits.

One of the special moments in my life occurred during an episode of juggling science and babies. In the days before James, Eddie and

I were riding a bus to Queensland, where I was to lead an Earthwatch expedition to study the canopy. It was not feasible either financially or morally in my situation to hire a sitter, so Eddie accompanied me on these infrequent research trips. For the bus ride I had packed a bag of kiddie treasures consisting of snacks, books, and other games to occupy the short attention span of a three-year-old. I had a new Dr. Seuss book, *Green Eggs and Ham*. Having taught Eddie all of the alphabet sounds, I handed the book over to him. Miraculously, he began to sound it out and proceeded to read the entire book. Not only did he read *Green Eggs and Ham,* but at the O'Reillys' rain-forest guest house he read the menu at every meal. I am not sure if my research colleagues shared in the awe of our miracle, but I was gratified to have the privilege of enjoying both parenthood and science. I did not forget that it was my scientific career that had led to that special day of reading on the bus together.

On a lesser note, poor Eddie paid a certain price for his mother's pursuits of plants. On that same trip he suffered bites on his ears from the sharp beaks of crimson rosellas (*Platycerus elegans,* family Platycercidae), and it took about six months for him to overcome his fear of large birds. He also suffered two bull-ant bites while exploring the natural world in our garden. These incidents seemed only to reinforce his conviction that he wanted to be a scientist. (I have since tried to encourage him to pursue more conventional occupations such as accounting or law, but to date he is still eager to follow in his mother's footsteps.)

Despite any criticism in my adopted culture of my pursuit of science, I did achieve one signal success: the procreation of two sons as heirs and future farmhands was a source of immense pride for my Australian husband. Still, children, like plants, require very special environmental conditions for growth. Was I capable of nurturing my sons in this outback world so alien to many of my childhood values?

5 The World's Greatest Lottery

*T*he forest is a vast laboratory in which new species are produced, tested, and eliminated if found defective. . . . These crowded seedlings springing up so hopefully beneath their towering parent; these ranks of spare and lean, undernourished young saplings; these tall middle-aged trees, already nudging at the shoulders of the dominating old fellows above them, telling them quietly that it is time to make way for a newer and more progressive generation — all are silently, endlessly vying with each other for a place in the sun.

— Alexander Skutch, *A Naturalist in Costa Rica,* 1971

Intermixed with my forays into the canopy, I became intimately involved in a second line of research on the forest floor, thanks to a wonderful mentor who "adopted" me during my first year as a graduate student. Joseph Connell, distinguished professor of biology at the University of California at Santa Barbara, came to Australia to ask questions about species diversity, a topic of strong theoretical and applied interest to both biologists and conservationists. Joe selected two ecosystems renowned for high species diversity to conduct field studies, tropical rain forests and coral reefs; and Queensland boasted both ecosystems in close proximity. A marine biologist by training, Joe needed a tropical botanist as collaborator. Because I was the only person studying rain-forest ecology at the University of Sydney, I had no competition for this coveted partnership. Joe remained a loyal colleague throughout my years of graduate study, and we continue to work together on this important project twenty years later.

Joe was truly one of the wonders of the ecological world, and he has influenced students worldwide. Since 1963, he and a group of assistants (I am his second generation of botanists, following after Leonard Webb and Geoff Tracey) have counted, identified, and mapped all the trees, saplings, and seedlings along marked transects in two Australian rain-forest plots. This long-term data collection is only now beginning to yield important results about which trees "make it to the top" and what influences their survival or mortality. Over several decades, many scientists worldwide have made pilgrimages to Australia to assist in our diversity project. Along our muddy rain-forest transects many new ecological theories have been postulated. An auxiliary correlation seemed to exist in our rain-forest fieldwork: the muddier the conditions, the more intellectual our musings. Among today's prominent scientists who spent time groveling for seedlings on these plots are Robert Black, Peter Chesson, Howard Choate, Laurel Fox, Katherine Gehring, Peter Green, David Lamb, Patrice Morrow, Donald Potts, Wayne Sousa, Tad Theimer, David Walter, and many others. "Winning the lottery" has two interpretations in this chapter — my good fortune in having Joe as a colleague, and the fate of seedlings on the rain-forest floor.

Although the majority of canopy dynamics were assumed to occur high above our heads, the forest floor was the birthplace of most of the action. It was there that one began to appreciate the incredible odds involved in the creation of a canopy tree. On the forest floor existed one of the world's greatest lotteries. Every canopy-tree species participated, in each phase of development from seeds to seedlings to juveniles to advanced regeneration. The odds were so dreadful that no gambler with any mathematical aptitude would play in this game. It has been estimated that as many as 150,000 seedlings may germinate annually in a hectare of rain forest. Of that crop, less than 1 percent will become tall trees. Our tropical rain-forest plots averaged 748 large trees (greater than 10 centimeters in diameter at breast height) per hectare, but sometimes more than two thousand seedlings germinated during one season.

Can seedlings increase their odds in this important ecological roulette, and if so, what factors influence the winners that reach the canopy? In this lottery, seeds must first successfully reach the forest floor or some crevice of soil to be eligible for germination. The descent from their birthplace in a fruit at the crown of a tree down through many layers of branches and understory foliage is fraught with hazards. If a seed makes it to the forest floor, it must either find suitable conditions for immediate germination or enter the seed bank (that is, remain intact in the soil without rotting or being eaten) to germinate at a later date.

The seedling lottery is not unlike the electronic computer games that my children love to play, whereby different levels or challenges must be overcome in order to win. In Nintendo, the character Mario continually faces obstacles and follows different paths in order to avoid fatality. For seeds that disperse from the canopy, five levels of challenge must be successfully achieved to "win":

1. Falling safely to the forest floor;
2. Germinating successfully;

3. Surviving the youthful (or cotyledon) stages and thereby attaining the status of advanced regeneration;
4. Existing in a suppressed state in the shade of the canopy and continuing to build up reserves as a subcanopy individual (for understory trees, this level is the final goal);
5. Eventually being released from a suppressed state by the sudden availability of light, and growing into a canopy tree.

Species that survive as saplings in the shade and wait for a gap are called *shade tolerant*. Some of our marked shade-tolerant seedlings are now thirty-five years old and still only 5 inches high. Their ability to exist on the shaded forest floor and "await" the formation of a gap is still one of the miracles of the botanical world, in my view. In contrast, other species are *shade intolerant,* meaning that they require sunlight for survival. These seedlings cannot survive if they germinate on the shaded forest floor, but grow very quickly if they happen to germinate in a sunny spot. Shade-intolerant species are often called *pioneer or colonizing species* because of their ability to grow successfully in the sunny conditions created after a disturbance. Over time, however, the shade-tolerant species grow slowly in the understory and often succeed those pioneer species, creating a new diversity of species in the canopy for the next generation. This is called *succession*.

The first stage in the lottery of the forest floor involves the movement of seeds from the top to the bottom. It may appear a simple act of gravity for seeds to float from their birthplace as part of a fruit to the forest floor below for germination, but this journey is hazardous. Consequently, trees have evolved innovative ways of enhancing the safety features of this journey. Different species of trees produce seeds that vary in size, weight, architecture, seasonality of dispersal, modes of attraction to engage couriers, and even different chemicals that protect the valuable cargo for its descent.

Flowers and fruits are most commonly formed in the upper canopies of trees, where tree growth is most vigorous. Wonderful exceptions exist, however, whereby plants bear fruits on their woody branches and trunks, termed *cauliflory*. So unusual was cauliflory to early explorers that when a Swedish botanist named Osbeck first observed it on a trunk in Java in 1752, he believed he had found a new species — a leafless parasite — and commented: "A small herb of barely a finger's length growing on tree trunks. It is so rare that so far as is known no one ever saw it before." Cauliflory is not common, and examples include bush honeysuckle (*Triunia youngiana,* family Proteaceae) in Australia, chocolate (*Theobroma cacao,* family Sterculiaceae) in South America, and the cannonball tree (*Couroupita guaianensis,* family Lecythidaceae) in Central America. My students — both children and adults — love to observe cauliflory, and to think about whether it looks like a cauliflower hanging from a tree trunk.

Seed rain is the term for the fall of seeds from the canopy to the forest floor. In temperate trees, flowering and fruiting occur regularly as an annual event. Oaks produce a crop of acorns every fall, and maples consistently send out showers of samaras in the spring, providing a goodly supply of helicopters for children in temperate regions to play with as they walk to school.

In the tropics, however, seed fall is much less predictable. Biologists do not yet understand the seasonal patterns of flowering and fruiting for many tropical canopy trees. Studies of the phenology of plants require many years of observation. Some reproductive phenologies have yielded huge surprises that have helped in the con-

---

→

Seedlings from the Australian rain forest. Present in all shapes and sizes, together they form a mosaic on the forest floor. Predicting which will eventually make it into the canopy is almost a lottery. Illustrations by Barbara Harrison.

Graptophyllum apingerum

Neolitsea dealbata

Orites excelsa

A. trifolialatum (seed)

Eugenia brachyandra

Geoissois benthaii

A. trifolialatum (seedling)

Argyrodendron trifoliolatum (advanced regeneration)

Cardwellia sublinis

Orites excelsa

Chrysophyllum sp.

4 cm

Wilkiea huegliana

servation of different species. For example, the Antarctic beech is a *mast seeder*. Every five years the beech canopies flower and fruit, and their seeds rain down throughout the cool temperate forest. Consequently, the weather conditions during the year of mast seed-fall are crucial to the germination of beeches. Because of this unusual behavior, the absence of seedlings during intermittent years is not necessarily a sign that beeches are declining.

When I first began studying Antarctic beeches, I spent many unsuccessful days searching in Australian montane rain forests under beech canopies for seedlings. After surveying thousands of square meters of forest floor under beech trees for several years, I found only two beech seedlings, both of which had survived on the fallen trunk of a tree fern (*Cyathea leichardti,* family Cyatheaceae). The texture of the *Cyathea* trunk provided a reasonable surface for germination and acted like a sponge, retaining more moisture than the soils. Initially, I was concerned about the apparent absence of seedlings. However, a period of twenty or thirty years without successful seed germination is probably not threatening for trees that purportedly live several thousand years. In addition, beeches also reproduce by suckers (or sprouts) from trunks or fallen trees, so their ability to perpetuate the next generation seems assured.

Why would a tree such as the beech have evolved as a mast seeder, when annual seed production seems less risky? Once again, it is not a simple matter of numbers of seeds produced. Biologists have found that seeds escape predators more easily when seed production is irregular. And in terms of energetics, annual seed production is expensive to the tree, usurping energy that could otherwise be utilized for foliage and production of energy via photosynthesis.

Like young boys, tree seeds come in an enormous range of sizes, from the cannonball tree (*Couroupita* sp., family Lecythidaceae) in Central America with a seed that is probably fatal if it lands on the head of a passer-by, to the nearly microscopic seeds of other tropical trees such as the giant stinging tree (*Dendrocnide excelsa,* family Urticaceae) that are wind dispersed. Seed size is a complex attribute. Large seeds obviously involve more of an investment by the parent tree for their production; but they also confer a larger probability of survival on each individual progeny. In contrast, smaller seeds are relatively inexpensive for a parent to produce but do not offer the seedlings any reserve energy to aid their establishment on the forest floor.

Small seeds produce small cotyledons (the first pair of leaves after germination), so they remain fragile as minute denizens of the forest floor. Small seeds are usually wind dispersed, resulting in seedling distribution that is widespread and random. Many small-seeded species germinate in gaps where light and moisture are plentiful. Because they have no food reserves, small seeds require optimum conditions for establishment.

Which is better, a large seed or a small seed? As a generalization, neither is better or worse, because in different situations either may be advantageous. On the rain-forest floor of Australia, the large seeds of the black bean (*Castanospermum australis,* family Fabaceae) and the coondoo trees (*Planchonella euphlebia,* family Sapotaceae) fall under the canopies of the parent trees, creating a situation whereby these species gradually dominate an entire stand. In other words, seedlings replace their parent trees with conspecifics. Some species such as the red apple (*Acmena ingens,* family Myrtaceae) have large, fleshy red seeds that are eaten by birds and small mammals, thereby being transported throughout the forest, rather than being clumped under the parent tree. Other small seeds disperse in the wind by the hundreds and thousands.

The fruits of the rain forest are many colored—purple, red, orange, lemon, flesh, white, black, mauve, pink, crimson, peach, and many variations in between. These bright colors serve to attract fruit-eating parrots and other predators who consume the flesh but pass the seeds through their digestive tract, acting as dispersers. One fascinating example is the fig bird *(Sphencotheres viridis,* family Oriolidae), which defecates fig seeds in the crotches of different canopy trees where it perches. The figs (*Ficus* sp., family Moraceae) germinate in the crowns of trees, extending their roots downward to the ground, rather than conventionally of sending shoots up to the canopy. This habit is termed hemiepiphytic, because the plants begin life as an epiphyte (air plant) but eventually extend down to root on the forest floor. The top-down pattern of fig growth is not only unique among rain-forest trees, but I privately believe it is destined to be the most successful pattern over evolutionary time. If only I could return to earth in one hundred thousand years to observe the rain forest! My prediction is that figs, with their innovative mode of securing a spot in full sunlight and then growing top downward, will dominate the forests.

Figs not only have a unique means of securing a canopy spot, but their ultimate success is further ensured by an ability to strangle their host tree. As the fig roots grow downward to the ground, they surround the host and expand, constricting the host tree until it dies and decays. Many strangler figs have hollow centers because the host decayed, leaving the fig to grow as a surrounding shell.

To study the seedlings on the forest floor required a type of grueling and repetitive fieldwork termed groveling by those of us involved with studies of this biological lottery. Optimist that I am, I likened seedling surveys with their rigorous up-and-down, sit-stand-squat motions to an aerobic physical fitness course, but without the extravagant fees. We spent many long days crawling along the forest floor to find, identify, and mark rain-forest seedlings. The mission was to measure the distribution and abundance of all

"Groveling" on the forest floor, which consists of crawling along to tag and measure every seedling. These tagged plants of *Planchonella* sp. are more than thirty years old as of our 1998 census. Such slow growth dramatically changes our views of rain-forest tree growth and re-generation. Photograph by Joseph Connell.

species of seedlings on our plots, then follow their progress over the years. Which died? Which were rare? Which grew but did not persist? Which persisted but did not grow? Which species eventually reached the canopy? This work required a long time frame and the patience to identify many, many tiny individuals. We used permanent aluminum tags, with numbers that now range beyond sixty thousand), and a grid system on the forest floor to map new seedlings and check out old recruits. The task was overwhelming, but led to an inevitable camaraderie or *esprit de corps* as we literally crawled along at a snail's pace, stopping for Oreo cookies or Minties (a favorite Aussie candy) after groveling for distances of 30 feet or so. It required so much concentration that a field partner of mine once allowed a leech to enter his eyeball, so intent was he on looking for seedlings. We had to take him to the hospital to have it removed, for the leech had sucked a blood meal and was too swollen to crawl back out of his eye.

After thirty-five years of annual surveys on 4 hectares of rain forests in Australia, the seedling teams have found a large variability in the patterns of seed rain, seedling germination, and growth of tropical trees. Mast seeding, annual seed production, and intermittent seed rain triggered by environmental conditions such as seasonal rains or high light were all successful patterns utilized by neighboring species. Some adult tree species never flowered or fruited during the thirty-five years of observations. For example, zygogynum (*Zygogynum semecarpoides,* family Winteraceae), rose marara (*Pseudoweinmannia lachnocarpa,* family Cunoniaceae) and galbulimima (*Galbulimima belgraveana,* family Hamantandraceae) were present as adults but no progeny have ever been found in our censuses. We hypothesized that these species typically flowered infrequently—perhaps every fifty years or more—or that subtle climatic changes had led to their sterility. Only patient observations will reveal these secrets of the great forest floor lottery.

My view of forests will never be the same after engaging in seedling research. Over several decades, each species has taken on distinct attributes. I dread seed rains of sassafras (*Doryphora sassafras,* family Monimiaceae) with their hundreds of densely packed seedlings. I cringe at the sight of new vine recruits (they are very hard to identify). I am thrilled at the rare discovery of a kauri pine (*Agathis robusta,* family Araucariaceae), or the sight of a prickly ash (*Orites excelsa,* family Proteaceae) whose toothed cotyledons make its identification unmistakable. The forms and patterns of seedlings were both fascinating and varied, and their ecological habits were unique.

As a female field biologist, my participation in this collaborative research project was often logistically more complicated than that of my male counterparts. I recall some crazy moments trying to main-

tain a foothold in ecology while dealing with the daily events of nursing, dirty diapers, colic, and the trauma of losing a dummy (the
Australian term for a baby's pacifier) in the forest. I once found Eddie
sleeping in his crib under a "flyblown" woolen baby blanket (that is,
it was crawling with maggots, a frequent situation because blowflies
lay their eggs in damp wool). Since a clothes dryer was not part of
my household, Eddie's blanket had not completely dried on the
clothesline during a rainy winter week. These and other events made
me fearful that I could not readily juggle science with an outback
lifestyle, even though I desperately wanted to embrace both.

In rural Australia the roles of men and women were fairly traditional. Once children were born, women spent the majority of their
time in child-related duties, along with kitchen management. As a
person with a doctoral degree who had worked much of her adult
life aspiring to become a scientist, I was not prepared for this abrupt
change. I kept a *Journal of Ecology* wedged between the pages of my
Women's Weekly, so that I could glance at scientific articles but *appear*
to be studying the latest hints in home decorating. (It sounds like relatively spineless behavior, but as a tired parent one soon learns to
minimize adversity.)

My mother-in-law was a woman who had followed the traditional
path. She frequently reminded me that she had given up her career
in kindergarten teaching, and that such sacrifice was part of her role
as the wife of a grazier. Although I had hoped to enlist her support
in my pursuit of research on a part-time basis, she seemed to be
strongly opposed to the idea. Was it regrets about her own past and
the dreams she never pursued, I wondered? Or was it simply the convictions of a different generation? She was often too busy to babysit
for her grandchildren, yet she must have realized that, with no immediate family on this continent, I was totally exhausted. I believe
in my heart that she wanted me to embrace motherhood as a full-

time occupation without attempting to pursue academics on the side. I spent many wakeful hours in my rural bed wondering how to please this intimidating woman who was my closest neighbor, for I urgently wanted her friendship. Unfortunately, I felt that I was a great disappointment to her. Our different philosophies were exemplified by the fact that she offered to babysit when I went to get my hair done, but not when I wanted to go to the university library.

In November 1985 Eddie, who was four months old, accompanied me to the rain forest for our annual seedling census. I could not leave him home, since I had no one else to look after him. His presence required extensive packing of toys, diapers, baby food, and other paraphernalia, in addition to the cameras, notebooks, tape measures, leech-proof trousers, boots, rain gear, and plastic bags that constituted my scientific equipment. Typical of the juggling act, my library ranged from tree identification keys and rain-forest volumes to *Pat the Bunny* and *Goodnight Moon*.

My participation in the seedling project was only possible because of the loyalty of my American colleagues and my parents, all of whom encouraged my devotion to science. Every so often my mother ventured all the way from upstate New York to accompany me on rain-forest expeditions and assist with child care. She entertained Eddie between nursing and naps, in exchange for the experience and adventure of travel (although I am not sure this was a fair trade). I feel sure that my mother had not intended to travel such distances to see her grandchildren, yet she sympathized with my struggle to use my many years of scientific training to some end. She once confronted a python on a rain-forest trail while walking the baby in his stroller—every other recollection of the forest for her pales in comparison. Even worse, this was Grandma's second encounter with Australian snakes. And one year my brother and his wife ventured from their contrasting world in New York to serve as child-tenders in the rain forest and on the farm. My brother recalls Eddie at the age of three explaining all the bird songs to him, including the scientific name of the birds! Eddie often rode in the car with me as I played (and replayed) my tapes of bird songs in order to learn their identity, and he memorized them more quickly than I. My children definitely had an unusual upbringing, and they grasped my passion of science as early as their toddler years. I could not have maintained both family and career without family assistance, even if it came from clear across the globe.

As I became more adept at balancing children and science, I learned the maternal talent of doing two things at once. In fact, I used to wonder if my brain was split in half, allowing one portion to do a technical task while the other was preoccupied with babies.

My brother Ed showing his nephew Eddie the wonders of the rain forest from a back-pack, while I measured seedlings. Photograph by Beth Weatherby.

Surely many women can empathize with this phenomenon. During our seedling surveys, I would identify seedlings for three-hour intervals, then dash from our field site to nurse the baby, hug him, and gulp down a big glass of water. Then I would rush back and identify all the unknown seedlings encountered during my absence, thereby keeping continuity in both science and babies. It was frantic, but it worked. At night Eddie slept in my bed so that he could nurse without waking me up and without crying, since the walls of the lodge were very thin. Even though I played a critical role in the project as seedling identifier, I always worried that my male colleagues might be dissatisfied with my mothering obligations. Parental duties are respected by most professions today, but back in the early 1980s I occasionally sensed disdain for trying to juggle family and career.

After seed rain and subsequent germination, seedlings must sustain themselves during their juvenile phases. Cotyledons emerge, followed by juvenile leaves. At this point seedlings often exist in the shade in a suppressed state, gradually building up reserves but without rapid vertical growth. Once they are established enough to tolerate moderate dry spells and slight physical damage, they have attained the status of advanced regeneration, which is similar to teenage in human development. The mortality between germination and advanced regeneration is staggering. Of 65,000 seedlings tagged in 3.7 hectares of Australian rain forest over thirty years, fewer than 6,000—less than 10 percent—have survived beyond the seedling phase. (And we have ignored all the vines, which may germinate more profusely than trees!) It is likely that fewer than 10 percent of these newly germinated seedlings actually live more than several weeks because of physical factors such as drying out, trampling by animals, and flooding. And fewer than 1 percent of those that survive to advance regeneration will ever reach the subcanopy or canopy.

Probably more than 600,000 individuals germinated on our rain-forest tract, most of which we never tagged because they died in the eleven months between our annual surveys.

Marauders in the woods, however, can decimate an entire generation of seedlings in several hours. Australian brush turkeys (*Alectura lathami,* family Megapodidae) once trampled a year's crop of seedlings during a brief excavation for grubs on the forest floor. A male turkey also raked up large numbers of seedlings (plus our tags) while constructing his nest, called a mound. In one turkey mound at Lamington National Park in Queensland, we found several hundred seedling tags that had been raked from many yards away. Brush turkey mounds consist of several tons of soil, sticks, and stones, that create a special incubation chamber for the eggs with the heat generated from the process of decay. The males not only build the mound but maintain it until the eggs hatch, an unusual pattern of paternal care. Males in charge of housewifery were an oddity in Australia, even if they were only scrub turkeys in the forest!

Other marauders include marsupials that browse on the forest floor, such as the pretty-faced wallaby (*Macropus parryi,* family Macropodidae), the bush rat (*Rattus fuscipes,* family Muridae), and the rare prehensile-tailed rat (*Pogonomys mollipilosus,* family Muridae); birds such as the log runner (*Orthonyx temminckii,* family Orthonychidae) and the cassowary (*Casuarius casuarius,* family Casuaridae) displace soil as well as seedlings in their quest for grubs and other tasty morsels. (Some of our most able-bodied field assistants have cringed in terror at the sight of a cassowary in the north Queensland field site. It is reputedly the most dangerous bird in the world, and uses its legs to strike other creatures.) Finally, seedlings that have attained advanced regeneration status can still suffer mortality from extreme physical conditions such as a prolonged dry spell, a chance invasion by a herbivore, or a rock slide that snaps off the main stem.

In the final phases of the seedling lottery, established seedlings on the forest floor require a physical space or light gap in which to grow. Shade-tolerant species survive in the shade for many decades, but eventually require light to attain canopy status. Shade-intolerant species do not germinate at the outset without some direct light. The rain forest is a patchwork of gaps. Large treefalls, individual branch falls, even the simple loss of a single palm frond significantly alter the light levels on the forest floor. The result is a substantial variety of environmental conditions on the forest floor that promote a diversity of species. Over our thirty-five years of seedling censuses, the mapping of forest gaps has contributed greatly to the understanding of seedling growth dynamics. Comparisons of seedlings in gap versus nongap situations show convincingly that seedlings require the chance event of gap formation in order to initiate rapid vertical growth. In the absence of a gap, some seedlings remain in a suppressed state with relatively little growth for many decades, awaiting an opportunity for light. Some individual seedlings of advanced regeneration status on our plots have passed their thirtieth birthday, yet are only 5 inches tall. How long can seedlings remain in this suppressed state in the shade? In the years to come, we hope to address this question.

What was the fate of thirty-five years of information on seedling recruitment, mortality, and growth? After it was entered into a large computer database, we assessed it for patterns and chaos. It was impossible to predict patterns of several hundred species, from casual observations. Some trees had adults but not juveniles of any other age class; for instance, the rose marara (*Pseudoweimmannia lachnocarpa,* family Cunoniaceae) and scrub turpentine (*Rhodamnia rubescens,* family Myrtaceae), all as difficult to pronounce as to locate on the forest floor! Other trees had adults and new recruits, but very few saplings: lignum vitae (*Premna lignum vitae,* family Verbeneceae) is an example. And some species were extremely rare, with few individuals of any age class; for example, the brown beech (*Pennantia cunninghamii,* family Icacinaceae) and twin-leaf tuckeroo (*Rhysotoechia bifoliolata,* family Sapindaceae). What will happen to these species? Will the remaining parent trees suddenly produce seeds? Will the species become locally extinct during our lifetime? Will the species that are now common (sassafras, booyong) someday become rare? The intricate patterns of growth and survival of common and rare species together constitute the future of the rain-forest canopy; many years of observation will be needed to unravel the data.

We take our seedling census every year, and we check the mature trees every five years. After several decades of data collection, we can now predict the phenology of fruiting events for different species; but it may take several centuries to fully quantify this complex forest-floor lottery. Although we cannot claim to have all the answers after only thirty-five years of data collection, we have begun to understand some of the mechanisms that contribute to the dynamics of canopy diversity, including seed size and dispersal, phenology, predators and pathogens, and chance. We know that a seedling 5 inches tall can be over thirty years old, a fact that certainly changes our perspective on rain-forest conservation. In parallel fashion, I have learned much about the infant and juvenile phases of young boys. Seedlings and children — both have provided joy and challenge to enrich my life.

6 Highways to Heaven

When I see birches bend to left and right
Across the lines of straighter darker trees,
I like to think some boy's been swinging them. . . .
Some boy too far from town to learn baseball,
Whose only play was what he found himself,
Summer or winter, and could play alone.
One by one he subdued his father's trees
By riding them down over and over again . . .
So was I once myself a swinger of birches.
And so I dream of going back to be. . . .
I'd like to get away from earth awhile
And then come back to it and begin over. . . .
I'd like to go by climbing a birch tree,
And climb black branches up a snow-white trunk
Toward heaven, till the tree could bear no more,
But dipped its top and set me down again.
That would be good both going and coming back.
One could do worse than be a swinger of birches.
— Robert Frost, "Birches," 1916

As children, we learn to love trees. We climb them, we build forts in their boughs, we lie on the grass beneath them and watch their branches sway in the wind, we envy monkeys and birds their agility, and we find fascination with the tiny beasts that inhabit decaying tree trunks. Perhaps strangest, we spend most of our time gazing in awe at trees from an extremely limited perspective: the ground. We gaze upward, attempting to sort out the complex array of branches and foliage that is difficult to observe and wondering what sorts of creatures inhabit the crevices beyond our reach.

When I returned from Australia to my position as a biology professor at Williams College, I wanted to share the wonders of the forest canopy with my enthusiastic biology students. To achieve this, I built a research "tree house" that was the perfect instrument to enable students to gain a sense of wonder for the canopy.

The trip across the Pacific Ocean seemed to last forever, especially traveling alone with two small children. Twice in previous years I had made this trip with two babies, so I was "relieved" to have toddlers instead. Eddie was five and James three. I kept my overnight vigil, traipsing to the toilet with first one and then the other, fetching juice and water and crackers, reading and rereading Dr. Seuss, trying to calculate how much of our fourteen-hour Pacific leg remained, opening the myriad small gifts I had carefully wrapped in bright paper to keep up the children's spirits and occupy their attention.

We arrived in Los Angeles at nine in the morning. A long walk through many hallways of under-construction customs areas must have been very discouraging to new immigrants. We reached customs only to find a lengthy queue of people that snaked around an enormous room like a dendritic river system. Still, I was so relieved to be on American soil that nothing could dampen my spirits. When I reached the customs desk, the young officer looked me straight in the eye and said "Welcome home." I burst into tears. The arduous voyage superimposed on my precarious emotional state elicited the response; only then did I realize how exhausted I was after several months of physical and emotional preparation.

The children and I had traveled from our sheep farm down to Sydney, crossed the Pacific, and then traversed the American continent in thirty-six straight hours of flying time, an ordeal for even the fittest adult but definitely challenging for a mother with two young boys. After many emotional upheavals, Andrew and I had decided to separate, on a temporary basis, so that I could put my passion for science to the test — did I really want a career in science or was it truly an unachievable dream?

I shall never forget the day in May 1989 when I received a telephone call from the biology department at Williams College asking me to be a visiting professor for six months. I secretly cried with joy. It wrenched my heart to feel such pride for this invitation to realize that it would be met with disdain and embarrassment by my Australian family. Nor shall I forget the moment when my husband, in front of his mother, gruffly told me that I could accept the invitation, but only because it would get "this academic stuff" out of my system. Despite the fact that my career was being ridiculed, I was overjoyed to have his reluctant blessing to embark on this challenge. My mother-in-law warned me that a good wife would never leave her husband alone in his bed, and I sadly realized that we would never see eye to eye on the definition of a "good" marriage. I do believe that she wanted to help me become a proper wife, but I simply could not play the traditional role and still be true to my inner self. I prayed that a six-month respite might make all of us more appreciative and tolerant of our differing perspectives. (The traumatic details of packing and maintaining some semblance of a normal home life prior to our departure remain locked in the secret pages of my diary.)

The children and I proceeded through Los Angeles customs and endured a four-hour layover until our next flight across the continental United States. I was elated to be embarking on a career track after my hard-earned academic training. There were a few drawbacks: I was now a single parent; I had left most of my physical belongings halfway around the globe; I was renting a house of unknown condition; I was bringing two small children into an entirely new culture, where even the language was difficult for them to understand; and I would receive a very modest wage that made us eligible for food stamps. These details seemed inconsequential in comparison to what we had left behind. We were safely in America, and it became our land of opportunity.

For several days after the long flight across the Pacific Ocean, the children slept back-to-front. They were awake at night and slept during the day. Eventually their body clocks straightened out. It was a beautiful Indian summer week in New England when we arrived in Massachusetts early in October 1990. I worried that the boys would miss their father, but they were busy taking in the sights and smells and sounds of a new country. Eddie, always the optimist, smiled and said, "We are a six-family now" — meaning me, Eddie, James, his maternal grandparents, and his Uncle Ed (the last three of whom he would get to know well for the first time in his life).

Sight unseen, we had rented a house near the college campus from a professor going on sabbatical. It seemed a practical solution, in that it offered furnished accommodation on relatively short notice. The rent was more than my wage, so I was not prepared for the derelict condition of the house. Still, not many options were available to a part-time professor in this small town. (I was too naive at the time to realize that professorial wages are negotiable.) The house was a real estate agent's dream, the kind described as having "a lot of potential for the handyman." One outside door continually blew open, and most of the windows had no screens or storm windows, except for a few sheets of plastic. My environmental ire was aroused when

I thought about the chill of a Massachusetts winter. The owner's definition of "furnished" was very different from ours. Each bedroom had a bed, but in some cases that simply meant a mattress on bricks. Worst of all, a healthy population of dust-bunnies populated every crevice and gave the boys runny noses. My parents had generously spent three days scrubbing and washing and vacuuming, which seemed to make only a minor dent in the "bunny" population. Worse, the majority of the kitchen utensils showed the historic remains of many mealtimes. (I was appalled to learn later that the professor's wife was a caterer and actually used her kitchenware professionally.) In addition to paying high rent and enormous heating costs, I bought dishes, blankets, and some furniture to make the boys feel comfortable in their new world.

Both Eddie and James, in their cheerful and fun-loving fashion, loved this monstrous, rambling, cold domicile. Their grandmother kindly bought them each a tricycle; the halls and living room, with their paucity of furniture and rugs, made an ideal riding kingdom. We quickly accumulated a mass of American hand-me-down toys and stored them in plastic milk crates which, when piled up, filled each boy's room with colorful pseudofurniture. I had some late-night battles with the plumbing and the electricity, but we survived.

Professors and other academics appear to be an anomaly in the human race. On the one hand, they are some of the most intelligent and gifted human beings on the planet, entrusted with the serious task of molding young minds and generating innovative ideas for the future. On the other hand, they often lack practical attributes. They suffer a relatively high incidence of personal mishap, endure precarious marriages and affairs, live in substandard conditions, have an obscure fascination for imaginative tinkering such as taping broken refrigerator doors shut, and tend to live between the library and the laundromat (even those who can afford a washing machine often retain a spartan student mentality). Some day I may write a book about the lifestyles of academics — it would be very colorful. As an academic, I am guilty of these eccentricities myself. But as a parent I hope to lift my standards, for the boys emulate my ways.

My first major task as a single parent reentering the workforce was to find child care for James. This was no easy task in a new town where I knew nothing about the reputation of the various programs and faced stiff competition for admittance. The most coveted program was College Day Care, which had a long waiting list. I put his name on the list and looked elsewhere. I found a church-based center that started at 7:00 A.M. and even served breakfast to families who might not have the time or money to give their children a nutritious start to the day. *And* it was only two blocks from our house. The floors were antiseptic linoleum and the playground was a grim, treeless area overlooking a major roadway; but the center had an immediate opening for James. It would be a temporary measure, so I continued to search elsewhere.

Eddie, meanwhile, was about to start first grade. He had already attended kindergarten and a few months of first grade in Australia, and his grasp of reading was at approximately fourth-grade level. I had deliberately enrolled him early in school in Australia to escape the tension within our household. It seemed logical to place him in first grade at the elementary school in Williamstown. Whereas Australians are not averse to sending their children to school at age five, Americans (especially in a college town) seem to advocate sending their children to school as late as possible, when they are six or almost seven. (It may be a competitive strategy, since a child will predictably perform better when he or she is older.) Eddie, at five, was significantly younger than his classmates. After quickly consulting with his new teachers, I decided to have him repeat kindergarten and thereby join a more homogeneous peer group. He spent a year learning cultural and emotional nuances rather than reading and writing, but it was a very positive experience for him.

During his first months he often came home from school without having eaten his lunch. When I inquired why, he replied that the other children kept him busy pronouncing words and phrases; everyone loved to hear his Australian accent. After the first week of school, we bought pumpkins and carved them. This was exciting for Australian boys who had never experienced Halloween before, except in their mother's storytelling. I became the best pumpkin carver on the block. We amassed an extensive collection of intricate cat, goblin, witch, and sun faces. As a single parent, I found myself trying to give 200 percent to my children, probably to compensate for the missing partner. Rather than feeling a void in their lives, the boys thrived on the constant devotion and love. Most important, our household was free of conflict.

Both boys made significant cultural adjustments with relative ease. The first time we went to the school playground, James came to me in tears. He was frightened by the complex play area, with its timber maze and slides and challenges. Never in his young life had he seen such a large and complicated toy. But that seemed to be his only moment of trauma in a month of enormous physical and emotional transition. He and Eddie slept and ate well, learned how to jump into leaf piles, and play soccer, and developed a taste for pizza, gourmet ice cream, zillions of choices of cereals, fresh corn on the cob, and pumpkin pie, to name but a few of the products that were new to them. Eddie, who had exhibited an eye twitch during his last year on the farm, soon lost this nervous habit.

Miraculously, a vacancy became available for James at the college day-care center. Early in our American life, his caregivers referred to James as the mayor of the school; he was in command of all the children and even the adults, but in a very kind and gentle fashion. I shall never forget receiving an urgent telephone call from his teacher asking whether James could recognize the nightshade plant (*Solanum dulcamara,* family Solanaceae). When I answered affirmatively, the school rushed another pupil off to the hospital to have his stomach pumped. The child had picked and eaten some deadly nightshade berries along the fence of the day-care playground. None of the teachers recognized the plant, but James warned them that it was poisonous and became a local hero.

Eddie had a runny nose that was exacerbated by our dusty household, so I took him to a pediatrician for a complete physical examination. With a quick analysis using a digital gadget we had never seen in Australia, the doctor diagnosed Eddie as having a 35 percent hearing reduction due to fluids. Poor guy! As I thought back to incidents when his father had punished him for not listening, I was not surprised to realize that perhaps Eddie's response had been caused by a physical limitation, not a defiance of authority.

We talked occasionally by telephone to the boys' father, often in the middle of the night owing to the time difference and the fact that he spent most of his daylight hours out with the livestock. Eddie and James both spoke with great enthusiasm about their new schools, friends, toys, and adventures in Massachusetts. When I asked their dad if he would try to come and spend some time with us, he replied that he had no interest in coming to the USA, no interest in seeing me, and no interest in seeing Williamstown. Perhaps I had been fooling myself by envisioning this separation as temporary. Perhaps the cultural attributes of our relationship were stronger than the marital bonds.

My first task as professor was to teach a "winter study," on a topic of my choice. I chose the controversies surrounding tropical rainforest conservation, including the social, economic, and political ramifications of tropical forest management. Most classes were held in my living room, to offer the students an environment conducive to discussion. Another year I taught a field biology course that included travel to Florida to visit coastal and hammock ecosystems. The students enjoyed the change from the Massachusetts weather!

When I was a student, winter study was my favorite academic experience — only one subject on which to focus, total immersion in a topic, the complete attention of a professor in a small class, and unique field opportunities. While still in Australia, I had taught a winter study for Williams students entitled Ecosystems of Australia. Fifteen students had flown over and spent one week in the rain forest, one week on the reef, and one week in the outback. It was a tremendous field opportunity for them, and a chance for me to focus on teaching field biology. It was also a special experience for my children, who were "adopted" by fifteen big brothers and sisters and transported with them to the reef and the rain forest. Although it always required extra planning to combine my children with my fieldwork, the end result was that James and Eddie's young lives were enriched by a plethora of special encounters with nature.

Life as a professor at Williams was demanding but rewarding. The students asked challenging questions and did not hesitate to request extra time for discussion, even if it meant calling me at home. I enjoyed the stimulation, however, and was excited to be part of this academic community. It was hard to believe that only several months before I had been on the farm in Australia daydreaming about this lifestyle. I was not disappointed in my dreams — the life was every bit as stimulating as I had imagined.

Our first month in Williamstown was marked by two encounters with famous writers. On December 4, 1990, I was invited to present a talk on my Australian canopy research to the biodiversity group at Harvard University headed by E. O. Wilson, a world-famous expert on biodiversity. It was an honor to meet and speak with this renowned biologist. His writing habits inspired me: his students claimed that every Monday he brought to the office several yellow writing tablets full of text, which his secretary then transcribed for him.

The second interaction involved Jill Ker Conway, who had recently written a best-selling memoir called *The Road from Coorain*. Jill candidly described her upbringing on a sheep station in Australia. In actual fact, Coorain is not far from our station, Ruby Hills; and some of my experiences in the Australian outback were very similar to hers of twenty years earlier. She discussed issues of gender in Australia and her eventual "escape" to America to find intellectual freedom as a female academic. (After leaving Australia, she became the president of Smith College.) Impulsively I sent a letter of thanks. I explained how much her book had meant to me, and to many of my female friends in rural Australia, and how it had inspired me to accept the temporary offer to be a visiting professor at Williams College. She immediately wrote back, advising me to seek a divorce and never to set foot on the farm again. She even gave me the name of her female lawyer in Amherst, Massachusetts. I was overwhelmed by her strong convictions and flattered by her sense of compassion for my situation.

Between Ed Wilson's wonderful descriptions of natural history and Jill Conway's graphic depiction of life in Australia, I began to think about writing a book of my own.

I taught Introduction to Environmental Studies (to more than a hundred students) and Advanced Plant Ecology (a laboratory course for approximately twenty biology majors). Some memorable incidents took place, as when a freshman selected the book *How to Shit in the Woods* for his environmental literature report, and some political problems, such as allegations of harassment by female students against a professor. But the life in a small academic community was blessed with a richness of ideas, creativity, and programs. It was the ultimate contrast from our rural outback existence, which seemed a world away.

When I look back on those first years of balancing motherhood with science, I can cite one major shortcoming: too little time allocated to self. My children blossomed, my career blossomed, but I had little or no time to develop a personal life or pursue a hobby or two. I resigned myself to addressing this personal void in a later chapter of my life.

In February my husband demanded that I break my contract with the college and return to Australia in March. "Enough is enough," he said. For me it was a simple decision. My sons and I were happy in our new situation, and I felt a strong need to honor my contract and complete the semester. My resolve to complete my contract did not meet with approval from Australia.

To commemorate this difficult decision and the traumatic phone calls that followed, I planned a short vacation. Like so many New Englanders, by late February we were feeling housebound. It seemed appropriate to organize a trip to Florida, to thaw out and to show the boys those coastal ecosystems. Once there, the boys loved the alligators and roseate spoonbills at the Ding Darling Sanctuary on Sanibel Island, the stork rookeries at Corkscrew Swamp, and a manatee swimming near Captiva Island. A Massachusetts college town may be stimulating, but there is nothing like the warmth of Florida in the winter.

Back at Williams, I wanted to take my Advanced Ecology students on a field trip. A bit of homework revealed that the University of Massachusetts had a field station on Nantucket Island, surrounded by interesting coastal and island ecosystems. To make possible such an undertaking, an old friend offered to accompany the expedition as a nanny for Eddie and James. On a brisk spring weekend in April, we took the ferry across Nantucket Sound. The sights and smells of the open sea were invigorating.

Cape Cod was one of the epicenters for Lyme disease, a tick-dispersed affliction that left people run-down, tired, and chronically ill. I must have been fearful about the combination of young people and ticks, because I awoke during the second night with ticks on my mind. Armed with a flashlight, I got out of bed and peered into James's bed, where he was sleeping peacefully. Without hesitation I placed my finger on the right side of his head behind his ear and found a tick feasting. Was it motherly instinct or just incredible luck? I shall never know how I happened to develop such a sixth sense for that tick, but the experience was sobering for all of my students. Ticks or no, we had a wonderful time exploring the ecosystems of Nantucket.

During my tenure as a professor of undergraduates, single-rope techniques for access into the forest canopy began to frustrate me. When I was a graduate student, they were ideal, inexpensive and relatively portable. As a teacher, however, I could not share the canopy with my students by using ropes, for only one person at a time could mount them. I taught students to climb, and we purchased several pieces of hardware for the ecology laboratory; but ropes remained limiting for class activities.

During the 1980s, when canopy research was still in its pioneering stages, canopy access was principally limited to solo efforts; single-rope techniques, ladders, and towers. Devices to facilitate research by a group of scientists simply did not exist, although several were in the development stage. Among the possibilities being examined were the French dirigible Radeau des Cimes (see Chapter 7), and the construction crane (see Chapter 8). Obviously, methods that allowed several scientists to work collaboratively tended to be more expensive than solo techniques.

Like a gift from heaven, a letter came to me one day from an arborist in nearby Amherst. He not only had expertise in construction and working in treetops, but he also had strong convictions about the conservation of tropical forests. Would I consider collaborating? Possibilities jumped into my mind — tree houses, tree bridges, tree platforms, tree rigging for research equipment. Would this person I had never met be willing to discuss my quixotic visions of canopy access?

He was willing. We met at 9:00 A.M. on January 30, 1991, and my "highways to heaven" concept was officially born.

Bart Bouricius and I brainstormed for several months about the design of our temperate-canopy walkway in Hopkins Forest, the Williams College research forest in northwestern Massachusetts. We received a small grant from a local foundation interested in environmental concerns. Our budget was a modest $2,500, which provided two platforms connected by one bridge with a 75-foot access ladder, plus safety equipment for the students. (We provided our labor gratis.) With a price tag less than that of most microscopes, the walkway proved an excellent investment for the advancement of science.

The walkway offers an alternative means of studying forest canopies in a relatively safe, permanent fashion. It thereby facilitated long-term collaborative studies that are not feasible with ropes. We designed a modular system of bridges and platforms as units that were individually priced, with the goal of repeating our building process in other forests. Working with an arborist builder expanded my horizons enormously. New words were added to my vocabulary: eyebolts, thimble eye lags, steel aircraft cable, galvanized steel sleeves, seizing wire, U-bolts, sling links, and more. All of these materials were part of Bart's recipe for building a solid, permanent, safe canopy structure.

Our construction was completed in May 1991. The weather was brisk, as the snow season was not yet over, and my fingers were con-

The first canopy walkway in North America, constructed at Williams College while I was a biology professor there. Students conducted original research, and several published their results, as a consequence of this new tool for canopy access. Photograph by Paul Clermont.

tinuously frozen. Bart did the main canopy construction work; I served as "dirt" (the builder's term for a worker who remains on the ground). We spent several weekends in the forest, using time away from our normal workweek. Because this was our first design, we measured everything with precision and kept careful track of costs. Bart became a familiar face at the local hardware outlets, as he selected all the bits and pieces with greatest care.

Our fastidiousness paid off. Two platforms connected by a 25-foot bridge were completed in about four weeks. We held a christening in the forest. The canopy scientist and photographer Mark Moffett came out from Harvard University and broke a bottle of champagne on the tree trunk, cut the ribbon on the ladder, and made a brief speech to the biology professors and students who attended. We all rejoiced in this new canopy-access technique and were eager to explore the upper regions of the otherwise familiar temperate forest.

Our structure might never have amounted to more than a glorified tree house, had it not been for the success of the research carried out by my students that season. My Advanced Ecology class had a large number of canopy enthusiasts, several of whom designed projects to work on through the summer in our "green laboratory." Students studied leaf growth, canopy phenology, small-mammal populations, insect diversity, wood growth, and even acid rain from our 75-foot perch.

One study in particular put Williams College's walkway on the canopy research map. Peter Taylor and Alexandra (Alex) Smith worked together trapping small mammals. Peter had read the studies of Jay Malcolm, who designed a special small-mammal trapping technique in the canopies of tropical Brazil. Jay's design used a pulley system to hoist a three-tiered trap into the canopy, thereby allowing replicated treetop sampling without climbing up and down each day. Determined to replicate this process in a temperate forest, Peter borrowed my car and bought timber, nails, and other supplies at the local hardware shop. After a day of sawing and nailing, he had produced four of the latest live-mammal trapping gadgets in the world.

The traps were a success. Not only did the students capture white-footed mice (*Peromyscus maniculatus* and *P. leucopus,* family Rodentia), but they also got flying squirrels. And not just northern flying squirrels as one would expect, but southern flying squirrels (*Glaucomys volans,* family Rodentia). These small mammals were previously unknown in the forests of northern Massachusetts, and flying squirrels in general were not well documented in this region. Significant to our results was the fact that flying squirrels are known to consume gypsy moths (*Lymantria dispar,* family Lymantriidae). Could it be that the students had discovered a new and important predator on the gypsy moth populations of New England? Because of our excitement about this idea, Peter decided to devote his senior thesis to answering the question.

After another season of sampling, Peter found that flying squirrels were relatively abundant in the oak-and-maple canopy of the college research forest, and that the predation of gypsy moth pupae in the canopy was significantly higher than at ground level. In situations where gypsy moth pupae were moderately abundant, the flying squirrel appeared to be a major predator in regulating the numbers of this formidable forest pest. Despite the millions of dollars that had been spent on gypsy moth research, no one had ever trapped small mammals or experimented with gypsy moth pupae above the convenient height of 6 feet. Peter was a pioneer, the first person to sample small mammals in the upper canopy of the New England woodlands, and consequently he made new discoveries in an otherwise well-known forest habitat. Here was a wonderful lesson in field ecology: we may think we know almost everything about our backyards (temperate forests, in this case), but we still may   know nothing about what lies just beyond.

I had an engrossing semester and was able to give my students some unusual opportunities to meet famous scientists. Since it was a novelty for me to be resident in the United States, not simply visiting for a week from far away, a number of my American colleagues came to visit. In most cases, their underlying mission was to persuade me not to return to rural Australia, where they perceived my lifestyle as incompatible with the pursuit of science. Regardless of their intent, it was marvelous to share them with my students. Among the visitors were Patrice Morrow, an expert on herbivory and plant stress; Jack Schultz, a renowned leaf chemist and expert on gypsy moths; his wife, Heidi Appel, an expert on caterpillar gut physiology; Hal Heatwole, my sea-snake supervisor and dieback colleague; Mark Moffett, the entomologist and acclaimed *National Geographic* photographer; and David Cottingham, an environmental affairs advocate at the White House. Some of my former Williams classmates also visited and participated in classroom discussions: John Cole, from the Environmental Protection Agency; Jan Goldman, who practiced environmental law; and Donald Weber, who studied with insect pests on crops. In addition to my students, my sons rejoiced in these interesting house guests who shared their love for bugs and other unusual creatures.

The seasonality of temperate forests was in stark contrast to the perpetual greenness of my Australian rain-forest research sites. After almost forty years, I was finally reversing my temperate bias. Twelve years in Australia had persuaded me that evergreen canopies were more commonplace than deciduous ones. But the simplicity of the Massachusetts seasonality was a relief. The leaves lasted only until October, so a data set on herbivory or leaf growth was complete in less than one year. It was possible to make annual comparisons without the complication of leaf age, as in the tropics. Better still, it was obvious that the insect herbivore populations plummeted to zero during the winter months, then grew exponentially during the brief summer period. Despite the fact that greater biodiversity of invertebrates existed in the tropical canopy, the explosion of caterpillar populations in the oak forests during July was incredible. The insects in a temperate forest were pulsed, with all their activity concentrated during a short peak; the insects in the tropics were relatively active throughout the year, but with lesser peaks during periods of leafing.

One of my students, Evan Preisser, compared insect diversity and abundance at the top and the bottom of the temperate forest canopy. Like the small-mammal studies, this relationship had not been addressed in temperate forests with modern methods of canopy access. Evan found that insects were more abundant near the forest floor of the temperate deciduous forests, whereas the Smithsonian entomologist Terry Erwin had shown that insects were more diverse in the tropical canopy. Presumably the temperate forest understory may offer a relatively benign physical climate that favors the survival of organisms as compared to its windy, more stressful canopy. In contrast, the tropical understory is too dark to foster high diversity, whereas its canopy boasts light and a high productivity level that attracts many organisms. More comparative studies of this nature are needed to understand fully which layers in which forests harbor the greatest diversity of life.

It was official. My friends from Australia informed me that my mother-in-law had found a substitute for me. The new woman in Andrew's life was evidently everything I was not, with definite priorities on the home front rather than aspirations in the professional world. Then too, the negative attitudes conveyed over the telephone from Australia convinced me that it was not appropriate to return to the farm. To clinch the decision, Williams offered me a one-year extension of my contract, this time with full salary. My teaching would be split between Environmental Studies and Biology, almost a dream come true. Within several days I had made my decision. The boys were happy and I was challenged. Andrew was obviously finding a new life that might be more harmonious with his parents' values, so the stress levels were lower for all of us. The situation was not perfect — I would like the boys to have a father, I would like to have a partner, and no doubt Andrew would like to see his sons — but it seemed at this point that no scenario could achieve all of our desires. I yearned to return to my cozy farmhouse where someone else would write the checks and fix the flat tires, but I desperately wanted respect for my passion for science. Maybe one more year would provide time enough for all of us to appreciate one another. Or maybe I was being naive again, and the year would only cause us to grow farther apart in our cultural and emotional values.

The walkway concept became very popular as a teaching and research tool throughout North America. Bart and I have since constructed walkways at several temperate sites: Hampshire College in Amherst, Massachusetts, for migrant bird research; Millbrook School in Millbrook, New York, for secondary-student canopy research; Coweeta Hydrological Reserve in North Carolina, for herbivory studies by the Institute of Ecology, University of Georgia; and Selby Botanical Gardens in Sarasota, Florida, for public education. We have mastered the concept of modular design, and our structures have proved weatherproof over almost a decade. We have expanded to tropical rain forests, with projects in Belize, Borneo, Ecuador, and others are pending in Costa Rica and Mexico.

In 1996 I traveled to the island of Savai'i in Western Samoa to assist in the design of a walkway for a rural village. Under the guidance of the ethnobotanist Paul Cox, the villagers planned a walkway for ecotourism, hoping to generate a small cash economy to help pay for their new school (a government-mandated building) instead of raising the funds through logging. The villagers, sensitive to the ecology of their rain forests, wanted to ensure that their children would inherit an intact rain forest. This concept of stewardship gave us hope for the future of island rain forests in the South Pacific.

Our network of walkways grows every year. Comparative studies are now possible in Australia, Samoa, North America, Central America, and South America. Even Africa boasts a walkway site in Uganda, although I have not yet been fortunate enough to visit it. I hope that over the next decade students can initiate additional comparative studies of canopy biology; the platforms and walkways will provide them with a relatively simple and safe method of canopy access.

7 On the Rooftop of the World

But all is out of reach of the curious and admiring naturalist. It is only over the outside of the great dome of verdure exposed to the vertical rays of the sun that flowers are produced, and on many of these trees there is not a single blossom to be found at a height less than a hundred feet. The whole glory of these forests could only be seen by sailing gently in a balloon over the undulating flowery surface above: such a treat is perhaps reserved for the traveler of a future age.

—Alfred Russell Wallace, *Travels on the Amazon,* 1848

My life as a field biologist reads somewhat like a fairy tale. One of my Earthwatch volunteers once sent me a card with the following quote: "Despite what you may think, my life is a true story!" Anyone who pursues an unconventional career has probably confronted this perception. I certainly have. Friends express amazement about my career experiences, and upon occasion I find myself sharing their disbelief. My participation in the Radeau des Cimes *("raft on top of the trees") in equatorial Africa during 1991 was one of those moments when I truly had to pinch myself. My childhood aspirations had come alive. I had traveled like Dorothy in* The Wizard of Oz!

When the children and I arrived from Australia to reside in rural Massachusetts, I looked forward to a more conventional lifestyle. Perhaps, however, that is impossible for a single parent teaching biology in a top liberal arts college, trying to juxtapose the rigors of research, lesson plans, intellectually challenging students who constantly call with questions, and a husband who occasionally phones from Australia to see if I have failed yet. What I definitely did not anticipate was that the "call of the tropics" would come back to haunt me.

In May 1991 a small advertisement in *Science* magazine caught my attention: "CANOPY MISSION SOCIETY announces a new CANOPY-RAFT assignment. The assignment is scheduled for September and October 1991 and will take place in the African rain forest. Scientists interested in participating in such an interdisciplinary operation should contact the organizers . . . "

It is impossible for anyone to hear about Francis Hallé's canopy treetop raft and dirigible without lapsing into childhood memories of tree climbing and balloons. Every child has visions of traveling in a balloon, and evidently Dr. Hallé was no exception. However, he made his dream a reality, not only for himself but also for many other scientists. He designed a hot-air balloom (or dirigible) to sail over the tree tops for research missions, and an inflatable platform (called a raft) for sampling the uppermost canopy. These two devices function jointly as the Radeau des Cimes rain-forest project, which has led to unprecedented collaborative research in the tropics. More on that later.

By June 1 my application had been submitted. An affirmative reply arrived on July 2. It took several weeks for the news to sink in. CAMEROON . . . AFRICA! The Biafran Congo Basin . . . malaria . . . pit vipers . . . research region of John and Terese Hart (biologists whom I very much admired) . . . army ants . . . *African Queen* and Humphrey Bogart . . . ebola virus . . . mbau stands in Zaire (translation: big, dominant trees of *Gilbertiodendron dewevrei,* family Caesalpiniaceae) . . . unexplored canopies with almost no literature on any aspect of their ecology, much less on insects in tree canopies. With all of the responsibilities that accompany daily life with children and class obligations, I barely had time to contemplate the adventures ahead.

As the chief scientist in charge of canopy herbivory for the expedition, I was entitled to bring two assistants. Mark Moffett, Harvard entomologist and canopy photographer extraordinaire, would come along to identify and photograph insect herbivores. Bruce Rinker, an enthusiastic secondary-school science teacher from Millbrook in upstate New York, would come as leaf-area measurer and collaborator on a canopy curriculum for high school biology classes.

At last, after four months devoted to details, we were ready. Supplies for all types of field conditions literally burst from our duffels: film, light traps, nets, batteries, vials, hammocks with attached mosquito netting, insect spray, more film, notebooks, alcohol, incontinence apparatus to keep in the sleeping hammock (in case the toilets were too far away for night navigation), first aid kit, more film, penetrometer to gauge leaf toughness, graph paper, prunes (just in case), Oreos (I practically inhale cookies to maintain my energy level when engaged in the physical rigors of field work), clippers, tweezers, a selection of field guides and scientific reprints to read during downpours, and more film.

The barrage of injections required to work in Africa nearly deterred me. However, it became a scientific exercise of sorts to find out what was needed, to time the injections in and around each other and in and around various academic and parental events, and to endure the painful aftermaths. All the expedition participants endured the following prophylaxis:

1. Mefloquine for malaria (oral dosage)
2. Yellow fever injection
3. Gamma globulin for hepatitis A (this shot was painful!)
4. Hepatitis B
5. Typhoid fever (two painful injections spaced a month apart; I began to realize that I did not like shots)
6. Tetanus (always recommended for travel to remote regions)
7. Cholera (two more painful injections a month apart; now I definitely knew that I did not like shots!!)

It seemed like excessive preparation for a twelve-day stay, but no one wanted to risk any of the diseases that Africa had to share. The recent outbreak of the deadly ebola virus in Zaire has given international attention to the potential problems of new diseases "escaping" from tropical regions. As of 1995, there was no known cure for ebola, which spreads through bodily fluids and kills 80 percent of those who contract it. The origin of the outbreak in Kikwit, Zaire, is ambiguous, but it may be that monkeys are carriers. Although most field biologists are dedicated to their work, all of us probably share a nagging, unspoken anxiety about the risk of disease when we work in the tropics.

This adventure would not have been possible for me without my parents' cheerful ability to live vicariously through their daughter's career. I was married to a man who was not able to allow his wife the freedom of her own career and who was immersed in a society that reinforced this view, so it was quite incredible to return to the United States and find support—even respect—for my research. Young women, who are often at the height of their careers intellectually, usually have the most "baggage": children, mortgages, college loans to repay, aging parents, and often spouses who are not sympathetic to female aspirations outside the home. My trip to Africa was the first botanical expedition that I had ever made without my children. Trips in Australia had included babies and child-care givers from my family in America—not an easy combination, but in that case the only compromise. The prospect of twelve days of uninterrupted field time was overwhelming, and I was grateful.

My parents had little fondness for my work in remote, tropical jungles, but fortunately accepted it with the blind devotion that parents often have for their offspring. They had been school teachers, where the biggest risk in their day was getting hit by a flying sandwich in the lunchroom. Both had been born and raised in Elmira, New York, and they had lived in the same stone house all their married lives. How could two such conservative and conventional parents produce a daughter who was to travel by hot-air balloon over the African jungle? It was a perpetual mystery among my family, and it remains an unanswered question. Fortunately for me, they accepted their share of responsibility in formulating my values and supported me logistically in my travels even though they did not share my passion for scientific pursuits. Their love for their grandchildren was such that I felt comfortable leaving the boys at home with them. I could not afford a nanny who would develop loyalty to our family, nor could I leave my children with casual sitters. I was often out of telephone contact, and this element of risk would have precluded any concentration on fieldwork.

Africa was the most remote and inaccessible destination to which I had ever ventured. I made a new will, took out a large life insurance policy, and got my father to cosign for my safe deposit box — all the procedures of a responsible single parent prior to departure for a remote location.

My colleague Bruce arrived from Millbrook on a brisk November morning to shuttle us both to the airport in Albany. Our third member, Mark, would fly from Boston and meet us in Paris. En route to the airport, Bruce and I indulged in a last-minute Western culinary decadence: three sticky buns from the supermarket bakery. (My other passion in life — besides science — is sweets.)

Our check-in was an ordeal typical of any field biologist, requiring lots of time and patience. Evidently no one at the Albany airport had ever packed an ultraviolet lamp (much less two) with wires connected to it, a whales-tail, or a large garden-insecticide sprayer as part of their international baggage. After thorough inspection, many questions, and detailed answers, we were checked through. Our first leg was flown on a tiny express plane, which had to offload four suitcases for weight reasons. Miraculously, our names were not drawn from a hat as the unlucky passengers forced to sacrifice baggage.

This venture into an unknown Africa was beyond comprehension. How can a vast land mass remain so unknown, so unexplored, so void of scientific discovery? During our four months of preparation, we had unearthed relatively little literature on the Biafran Congo rain-forest basin. The Campo Faunal Reserve in southern Cameroon was nothing but a dot on the map representing our destination, yet this region was considered one of the most colorful and diverse in the tropical world. Gerald Durrell eloquently described the virtues of Cameroon wildlife and his travels there in the 1950s; little other published material could be found.

I was looking to comparing this third continent, Africa, with the other two major tropical rain-forest regions (the Old World or Indo-Malaysian region, and the New World or neotropical region). For such intercontinental comparison is one of my lifelong aspirations. For over ten years I had been carefully documenting the herbivory in canopies of Old World tropical-forest tree species, finding that young shade leaves are defoliated more fully than old sun leaves. I had measured the qualities of leaf tissue that render them more (or less) susceptible to being eaten. Now, at long last, I had an opportunity to determine whether the same trends hold true on another continent.

Next stop Paris. We spent twelve hours there, awaiting our connection to Cameroon. The stopover was a lesson in economics. We took a taxi to the Louvre and were overcharged, but because we were unable to translate francs into dollars we happily paid the inflated fare. It was only inside the museum, when we had no money left to pay for admission, that we realized our error. We cashed some additional traveler's checks and enjoyed the "Mona Lisa" and other art treasures despite our mistake.

Tired, we returned to the airport and waited for our evening flight to Douala, the industrial capital of Cameroon. We played our favorite game, "Spot the Scientist." Alerted via fax messages that at least two other scientists were on our flight, we examined each passenger carefully for the requisite baggy pants, old brown laced shoes, and dirty backpack. Our game was unsuccessful, but we boarded eagerly.

The Douala International Airport had absolutely no lights to mark its approach, and I was convinced we were landing on a remote

African savannah. It was six in the morning and very dark — the tropics in winter. Military officials checked our bags, and it was hot and humid even in these early hours. Like many tropical ports of entry, this one did not seem to be somewhere a woman should arrive alone. The terminal was swarming with military personnel; others eagerly tried to carry our bags or offered a taxi ride at unregulated prices. We had been cautioned by our host to look at and speak to no one, and to keep our hands and eyes on our belongings at all times.

The three of us boarded a minibus supplied by Elf Oil company (sponsors of the expedition) and were driven through some depressed sections of town. Squat huts, camouflage-outfitted guards outside factory gates, and feral dogs sniffing trash attested to the state of unrest in this industrial city. Cameroon was undergoing a period of political upheaval, with the military in control and the government experiencing little stability.

We were deposited at dawn in a house surrounded by a strong wall, to await the awakening of the resident researchers who were returning to the States on the next flight. To my surprise, they included my friend Yves Basset, whom I had taught to climb trees in the Australian rain forest years ago when he was a graduate student. The scientific community shrinks with each passing year, as I continue to meet people from different continents. Gradually an intellectual spiderweb is created that interconnects many of us. I seem to be part of the last generation of scientists whose network was generated mostly by personal contact. Today networking requires only a computer to establish quick and frequent communication via e-mail. In the future, colleagues may not have to meet with one another to collaborate; biologists may even find it possible to work together in the field without going outside their offices (via remote cameras such as those in Chapter 8). But these technological advances will eliminate the valuable rapport that can only derive from shared experiences.

Working side by side in remote situations certainly strengthens personal ties with colleagues, and one picks field companions with utmost consideration when faced with the prospect of living and working together in remote jungles. Computer networking — though convenient and efficient — reduces these personal interactions, and will no doubt create a different type of rapport among scientists.

We waited several hours before departing for the jungle. Douala's industries had experienced intermittent strikes for more than nine months, we were told. People worked only on Saturday, so the streets were quiet and little was accomplished. Roland, our driver and the logistics officer for Operation Canopée, had a long list of jobs to complete for the camp, but he was frustrated by the strike. Faxes and phone calls were not expedited because no telephone operators were on duty, an electrical component could not be purchased to repair the new chair intended to lift people up to the raft (it had stopped working on day 2), malaria tablets were needed for a forgetful scientist who had left his at home. It was a set of impossible tasks in this paralyzed city. And so we sat, prisoners in a rented house, and listened to the sounds outside our walls of Cameroonian children playing in the streets, men fixing old cars, women sweeping and hanging out wash. A few urban birds chirped — mainly starlings, a few silver-eyes, and an unknown with the coloration of what is known to American birders as a CFW (a confusing fall warbler).

Our drive to the camp was incredible, a trip of stark contrasts. With a modern four-wheel-drive Mitsubishi vastly overpacked with luggage and people, we looked fairly ostentatious as we zipped along a highway at 140 kph (kilometers per hour). The restless atmosphere of urban poverty soon gave way to an impoverished rural population outside the city. People used the highway as a major walking path, exploiting every roadside resource as they walked. Wood, cane, and debris were collected in little two-wheeled carts. It was terrifying to speed along at a minimum of 100 kph with people thronging both sides of the vehicle. At dusk, the children got out of school and joined the stream of walkers. There were six police checks along the way. Roland requested that I occupy the front seat because he believed the presence of a woman would encourage the police to remain civil and not detain us. It worked — one of the few times my gender was an asset in conditions of remote fieldwork.

At the seaside resort of Kribi we turned onto a narrow dirt road, where the landscape became agrarian. Candles were lit in every hut, and I caught fleeting glimpses of shadowy faces around the evening meal. The landscape took on an almost magical aura with the small intermittent clusters of flame. Some people had candles on outside tables as they ate, and I could almost feel their relaxation permeate the humid air.

We finally arrived at the camp. Operation Canopée was also aglow with lights, but noisy gasoline generators, not quiet candles, were the source of power. The scene was reminiscent of a jungle movie, with thatched huts in a forest clearing. The camp was in its second month of operation when we arrived. That night almost fifty people were in residence, of whom ten would depart the next day. So we literally bumped bottoms, setting up our hammocks in a long line under the roof of the sleeping hut. A dashing, muscular Frenchman looked aghast when I slung my hammock next to his. He was obviously less than enthusiastic about a female intruding on his monastic tree-climbing adventure, but fortunately I could not understand his dismayed comments in rapid French. It was a strange sensation to hear people speaking so many languages in the middle of the African equatorial jungle — French, German, Japanese, and English. The only common thread was a sense of adventure in canopy science.

The first night in a sleeping hammock is like a fraternity initiation, a pointless exercise that (some) people are willing to endure. I remember looking at my watch at 11:30, 12:30, and 1:30 and musing at the concert, a unique symphony of forty-six snoring men strung up in hammocks and sleeping on their backs! Fortunately the hammock environment was bugless, for we had all brought mosquito netting to protect ourselves. There were three other women, all leaving on the morrow. I would be the only female during the next two-week stint.

The sounds of the African forest at night were astonishing: night-jars, frogs, cicadas, and many insects whose identities remained un-known. In the morning, the raucous calls of hornbills were accom-panied by their noisy wings whirring with every stroke. Hornbills are important components of the African rain-forest ecosystem. More than 70 percent of the West African rain-forest trees are re-puted to produce pulpy fruit, most of which is dispersed by these conspicuous birds. Contrary to coevolutionary expectations, there is not just one hornbill species adapted to eat each specific fruit size. Rather, the hornbills are opportunistic, several species often feeding together (or with monkeys) on ripe fruits in the canopy of a card-board tree (*Pycnanthus angolensis,* family Myristicaceae). With their oversized beaks, hornbills procure an abundance of fruits and then fly to a thicket to ingest their accumulated booty. The birds digest only the juicy pulp (termed arillus); the seeds pass unharmed through the intestines and are deposited onto the soil with the bird droppings.

Not unlike those of the hornbills, our meals at camp were also fairly raucous affairs. The food was extremely variable, and quality was strongly correlated with the intervals between supply trucks. Toward the end of a week, we often had unidentifiable meat with potatoes and gravy on top. One night we recognized the surface pockmarks of tongues, but were not sure from what animal the tongues had come. There were guesses about what other anatomical parts were eaten, but most of these were pure speculation (at least we hoped so). When the supply trucks arrived, however, dishes as elegant as garlic shrimp and steak with avocado were served. The cooks were not pastry chefs, although they did once attempt a chocolate pudding which had to be served in cups as a sweet, thick cocoa. American doctors had advised us not to eat lettuce or anything else that had been washed, but we could not resist; the salads were delicious, and the local lettuce was similar to, but better than, our Boston lettuce. I managed to escape the penalty associated with eating foods washed in the local water, but not everyone was so lucky. To suffer an intestinal bout in remote tropical Africa restricted the unlucky scientist to periods of lying in his hammock interspersed with frequent visits to the latrine — not a pleasant way to spend one's limited days at the site.

I was very careful about insect bites, wearing long sleeves and continually applying liberal amounts of bug spray. I had hoped with such prophylactic measures to avoid continual attack by disease vectors that included flies, mosquitoes and other UFOs. Unfortunately I was bitten twice by the yellow-eyed deer fly during my only vulnerable moments — in the shower. This fly is the carrier of river blindness, another debilitating tropical disease, but my colleagues assured me that only half of the flies were reputed to carry it. A small consolation!

As the only female in an otherwise male camp, I found showering to be a real challenge, not only because of insects but also because of staff intrusions. I probably became a prime educator of the local Pygmy assistants on American female anatomy and ablutions. My Western colleagues were amused that whenever I headed for the shower cubicles with my towel, an attentive group of ground staff would follow. Their most common ploy was to clamber upon the hot tin roof, as if to check the water hoses, and then peer over the edge into my stall. Once they brought machetes and proceeded to cut the grass just outside the shower stalls — all ten or so blades that had resisted the continual trampling. Getting dressed in the morning was another challenge, one that I accepted as a liability of the situation.

Then there was the matter of my underwear. Alas, it disappeared day by day, and we speculated that it must be adorning the bodies of the nearby village wives. I hope that is the case, and that they are pleased with my selection. A funny incident occurred during our last week, when an enormous and sad-looking pair of women's panties appeared in my hammock, presumably found somewhere in the camp and assumed to be mine. This underwear had probably been rejected by the Pygmy wives because of its large circumference, so it was tossed from hammock to hammock in camp, causing uproarious laughter among the fraternity of men.

The Pygmies from the nearby village walked through camp every day and back to their village, loads of wood balanced beautifully on their heads. Despite the theory that African rain forests may have been the site of our early human ancestors, these regions were not widely colonized until the last one thousand years. Shifting agriculture and the use of fire to clear forest pockets were relatively new practices in West Africa and probably had very little impact on the vegetation history. For their food the Pygmies relied largely on hunting. Their weapons included snares, bows and arrows, and spears. In fact, we did not venture onto the forest trails without a local guide, because our Western eyes were not trained to recognize the camouflaged snares set at irregular intervals. The forests provided a notable hunting ground, as well as a source of fruits, nuts, spices, fibers, and medicinal products.

Recent efforts to document ethnobotany in Africa have been limited, compared to some of the large-scale investigations in Central and South America. In the early 1900s, however, a Scottish doctor-botanist, J. M. Dalziel, identified over nine hundred genera of useful plants in West Africa. Traditional knowledge of plants for medicine and other products continues to be an important heritage of the African people. The Centre for the Study of Medicinal Plants in Cameroon has undertaken an inventory of medicinal plants. In a continent with virulent diseases such as malaria and AIDS, tropical plant remedies may yield vital solutions to future medical challenges. For example, the guinea worm that infects many Africans and visitors can be expelled by the application of a poultice from the leaves of the shrub *Combretum mucronatum* (family Combretaceae).

The Pygmy village near our camp was experiencing several cases of malaria. Our camp doctor, François Mgrel, who was blessedly free of duties, distributed tablets and engendered the friendship of the entire district. One child had a facial lymphoma. The doctor persuaded her family to allow him to photograph the cancerous outgrowth, in order to seek advice from physicians in Paris. Photography was a delicate issue with the Pygmies; pictures of married women were forbidden, as they were reputed to interfere with fertility.

Because he had so much leisure time, the doctor set up a remarkable badminton court and was willing to play anyone at any time. The local people, who loved to watch, found it hilarious to see white people chasing a delicate plastic "birdie."

One of the camp cooks, a local and someone whom I considered a friend, offered to take me to the nearby village so that I might better know the culture and conditions. He had an ulterior motive, however, to show the village his newest possession—me! Fortunately I was able to convince another male scientist to come along as chaperone. The village had a dirt track through the middle, with cabins on either side. In the center was the school and a small shop. The schoolchildren were delighted when I took their photos, and they appreciated the candy and pencils we brought as gifts. We went into all three classrooms, and in each one the students stood up respectfully when their teacher entered. The classrooms had dirt floors, hard benches, and one blackboard with several pieces of chalk as their only tools. Our Western education, in stark contrast, has become adorned with gadgets and trappings. It is hard to believe that these children daily spent from nine o'clock until noon, and from two to five o'clock in school. I wished that I had more to give the children than my boxes of pencils, yet I was somehow envious at the absence of Nintendo and Lego in their lives.

The dirigible was launched daily at 6:00 A.M., weather and health of crew permitting. A launch pad had been carved out in the forest and was covered with a plastic tarpaulin to cushion the huge balloon. Entry onto the tarp was permitted only with bare feet. The French have a wonderfully casual sense of organization; everything got done with nothing like the fuss or stress that might occur if Americans were shouting orders and organizational advice to one another. Two Africans held the ropes in front while Danny, the pilot, fired up a small flame just under the dirigible. A tiny balloon was always released first, to test wind conditions: a lovely combination of high and low technology. Finally, liftoff! The colorful balloon sailed quietly over the tips of the umbrella trees (*Musanga cecropioides,* family Cecropiaeae) that edged the clearing, then ventured out over the vast sea of green.

Very little is known about the African tropical rain forest. Insect fogging has never been performed on the equatorial forests there, although this popular method of investigating arthropod biodiversity has been utilized in many other regions. As an island continent, Africa is reputed to contain pockets, or refuges, of unique endemic species. But as the dimensions of tropical forest in Africa shrink, these cen-

The Radeau des Cimes designed by French researchers, perhaps the most innovative and colorful canopy-access tool in existence. In Cameroon, I used the dirigible and canopy sled (towed beneath the balloon) to survey herbivores in the uppermost canopy. Photograph by author.

ters of endemism become threatened, creating a powerful urgency to study the African tropics before they disappear.

Our canopy expedition was the first collaborative project in this region of equatorial Africa. A large majority of our findings will doubtless embody new records for science. This pioneering sense kept the morale of the scientists very high, despite minor setbacks such as diarrhea, the absence of amenities (electric lights, fans, ice), equipment failures, and sheer exhaustion from vertical rope climbing in the tropical heat and humidity.

The energy exerted simply to walk along the trails around camp was immense. After several minutes even the most athletic physique was bathed in sweat. My imported supply of Oreo cookies sustained me between meals, especially through the mornings when the

French breakfast of crusty bread and black coffee proved quite inadequate for my metabolism. The canopy raft was situated approximately 2 kilometers from camp atop a tall stand of trees; we hiked to it during our first day. I found it difficult to see the red and yellow structure over the uppermost branches, not only because it was so high above us, but also because my glasses were badly fogged after our walk. Once the condensation caused by my perspiration cleared, I saw a long snakelike rope suspended through a cathedral opening in the trees — our conduit to the world above.

The rope extended 55 meters, the distance from ground level to the raft above. Mark climbed first, toting his heavy camera bag and becoming too short of breath to exclaim about the incredible views. I went next, and the climb seemed never ending — past an African beehive, past several lianas, past several understory trees whose leaves I could not resist sampling, and finally through the porthole of the raft on top of the canopy. After climbing the equivalent of an eighteen-story building, I collapsed from exhaustion onto the mesh floor and spent several minutes basking in the ever-so-slight cool breeze that was wafting up from the understory.

The raft looked and felt like a giant inflatable ship: it creaked and rolled with the wind, and featured ropes and nautical cleats. Cleverly designed pockets on the tubing stored equipment and prevented our gear from falling "overboard." Bruce, who climbed third, suffered a mild attack of acrophobia, which is not unusual on a first ascent into the forest canopy. We urged him to spend his entire day sitting in one place, rather than leaping around the bouncy structure as Mark and I did. Bruce served as our clearinghouse for insect sorting and labeling. The temperature was well over 100°F above the canopy. We had not brought enough water even to last through the morning, and consequently all of us became extremely dehydrated. I suffered heat prostration, as evidenced by nausea and a severe headache (and had

The canopy raft. Lifted by the dirigible and placed atop different tree crowns, it facilitates semipermanent access, much the way a space station does. I am barely visible coming through the porthole on a rope, having climbed from the forest floor into the raft to measure leaves for insect damage. The sled shown in the previous photo is simply one section of this larger raft. Photograph by H. Bruce Rinker.

to retire to my hammock that afternoon with water and Oreos to recover).

The upper canopy is also stressful for animals and plants. Yves Basset, in his sampling of canopy insects, found very little diversity or abundance above the canopy as compared to within. And certainly birds and mammals were almost nonexistent in this rooftop of the world. The leaves in the uppermost canopy were well adapted to their harsh environment of sun, wind, and continual storms. Extremely tough and small in size, they boasted high photosynthetic rates, as measured by our colleague Rainer Lösch from Germany. In contrast, the understory leaves contributed less photosynthesis to the energetics of the entire tree, owing to the low light levels. Nevertheless, they were much preferred by insects and their surfaces were riddled with telltale holes from herbivores. In fact, the leaves in the canopy (sun leaves) are physically and physiologically often more different from the understory (shade leaves) of the same tree than they are from an entirely different species of tree. Characteristics of sun leaves, in comparison to shade leaves, include smaller size, greater toughness, lower water content, lighter green coloration, a higher rate of photosynthesis, and a shorter lifespan.

Why do insects prefer to consume shade leaves rather than sun leaves? Is it because they are softer and more palatable? Or is it merely that more foliage-feeding insects live in the understory than in the upper canopy? Access to the canopy, made possible through innovative devices like the raft, will enable scientists to answer these crucial questions, and others that will no doubt be raised as the result of further canopy studies.

Descent from the raft was a marvelous sensation. After our unbelievably laborious ascent, our climb down on the single rope was rapid and effortless. The use of a whales-tail allowed a smooth and safe "ride" down to the forest floor in a matter of minutes. With temperatures cooling and visions of a wonderful dinner dancing in our heads, we stumbled back along the trail and headed for the showers. After a long day in the canopy's world of hot, unyielding sunlight, and despite the fact that my body was hot, sticky and coated with the dust of crumbling bark, humus, and insect frass, I still was reluctant to step under the dribble of the cold shower. The fact that the water was untreated and pumped from an unseen source added to my hesitation. But field biologists get used to these risks, and the notion of a shower won out over the possibility of inadvertently gulping a mouthful of contaminated water.

I spent several afternoons analyzing leaves in the field lab. We measured leaf area, length, weight, and toughness, using techniques that were portable enough to endure the primitive conditions of a remote African rain forest. Little had we anticipated that our field lab would boast not only a state-of-the-art Sun minicomputer capable of digitizing leaf areas, but also a full-time technician to operate it for us. Both the computer and the technician were made available to scientists throughout the expedition. I had never before experienced such sophisticated data collection in remote field conditions.

Others were less fortunate in carrying out their field projects, because the physical conditions would not support some of the more delicate equipment. The Max Planck Institute in Germany had shipped 1,300 kilograms of luggage, including many expensive scientific instruments, to study the atmosphere above the canopy. Their equipment remained in customs at Douala, awaiting the appropriate paperwork (or bribes, perhaps) to be released. When it finally did arrive, only days before the German scientists were due to depart, they set up a tentful of wires, dials, gas bottles, and instrumentation, creating their own analytical lab. In theory, it was an exciting project; in reality, it was a nightmare of broken parts and German expletives. Their attempts were herculean, and their work on the atmosphere above the canopy represented a dramatic, unknown, and important frontier of research.

Our second day on the raft was much less traumatic than the first, because we had a better idea of what to expect. Bruce elected to stay at camp and work on understory leaves. I took along two six-packs of bottled water, plus my beloved Oreos for sustenance. Mark and I also carried a variety of devices for sampling insect herbivores in the canopy: sweep nets, beating trays, vials, tweezers, and insect fogging apparatus. We invented a new technique called minifogging, in that we sampled individual cubic meters of foliage adjacent to the raft.

This procedure should more accurately be called misting, because the droplet size was larger than typically employed in fogging. Our new samples were much smaller than those from the standard ground-based technique we had used previously, but the replication enabled us to sample ecologically comparable units at various sites.

We sampled in tree species that I had never before encountered. *Dialium pachyphyllum* (family Caesalpiniaceae) and *Sacoglottis gabonensis* (family Humiriaceae) were dominant at this site. Both had leaves of an elongate elliptical shape with entire edges, relatively sclerophyllous texture, and drip tips. After heavy rains, drip tips are thought to expedite the flow of water from the leaf surface, allowing the phylloplane to dry quickly. This minimizes the growth of epiphylly on the surface of the leaf, and also facilitates the downward flow of water to the roots below. In the course of our ten-day study, we sampled twenty-eight different tree species, and measured more than twelve hundred individual leaves. All of the herbivores we collected were counted and processed for identification by Mark back in the laboratory at the Museum of Comparative Zoology of Harvard University.

An unexpected personal success of the expedition was my bladder. Miraculously, I did not have to trek to the latrine in the middle of the night, not even once. As any mother can appreciate, my bladder had lost its endurance after childbirth. There probably were three primary reasons for its physiological success on this trip: the humidity and heat caused most of my bodily fluids to be shed through perspiration, the position of my body cramped in a hammock minimized pressure on the bladder, and the fear of stepping on the aggressive driver ants in the dark dampened my enthusiasm for midnight perambulations. We frequently saw highways of these marauding ants on their way to the toilets at dusk. Presumably they were raiding the pits to obtain their dinner.

The driver ants (*Dorylus* sp., similar in behavior to army ants in the neotropics) were one of the marvels of the African forest. They traveled fast and always appeared frenzied to get to their destination. Often several streams would charge along, one on top of the other, in different directions. A Pygmy showed us a large mammal that had been caught in one of his nearby snares. Unfortunately for him, driver ants had discovered the carcass first and the animal's body appeared to be torn in two, leaving only bones where the waves of ants had traveled across and consumed all flesh in their path. What a cruel death for that creature, and what a disaster for the Pygmy and his family, who lost their dinner to the ants' voracious attack.

Ants were paramount in the African lowland-forest ecosystem. They dominated ground-level dynamics, and several species were common in the canopy. We looked at several ant-plants: *Delpydora* sp. (family Sapotaceae) with its hairy petioles and caverns in which ants could find shelter, and cola bush (*Cola marsupium,* family Sterculiaceae) with its pouches. Ant-plants offer shelter and food to ant colonies, in exchange for protection from herbivores. In the treetops people continually complained about ant bites. So many ants lived in the canopy that one could not avoid knocking down nests while moving around the raft; inevitably the ants became agitated and inflicted their stinging bites on any and all available scientists. Many ant bites have left a permanent legacy of respect etched in my own memory. I cannot help but admire the voracity of these tiny creatures that attack beings thousands of times larger than they— and win!

Mark found an unusual ant on our first day and was convinced it might be a new species of *Oecophylla* (a pantropical genus in which no new species has been discovered in several hundred years). We frantically sampled ant nests and preserved some specimens in alcohol. Mark took literally hundreds of photos for documentation.

Bruce, in his Darwinian fashion, predicted that a new ant species would have a corresponding (and therefore also undiscovered) species of ant-mimicking spider living nearby. Sure enough, a small search yielded several pockets of silk, with the ant-mimics nestled inside. These spiders looked exactly like ants except that they had four pairs of legs (and of course, spinnerets and a few other less obvious features). One spider jumped from its silky hideout, grabbed an unsuspecting ant, and returned home to devour it. The spider was extremely quick because if other ants saw it, they would attack and kill the invader. What dramas played out in the ant colony! Nestled in the canopy, the ant nests looked like bunches of dead leaves, but they were so much more.

A villager brought in a gorilla skull, with the hope of selling it. Bruce would have liked it for the Millbrook School collection, but his conservation ethic plus the risk of bringing an endangered species through U.S. customs removed him from temptation. The villager claimed that the gorilla had attacked him and showed us wounds on his leg that allegedly were made by the animal. Its cranium had several machete cuts where the villager had whacked it to death. His story incited fierce debate among the scientists. Would a gorilla attack a person in this fashion, or was the story an alibi created to justify an attempt to sell an endangered species?

My sleeping bag and hammock were beginning to feel sticky as we began our second week of life in the jungle. I woke up several times with large welts on my leg, a consequence of falling asleep on my flashlight. Life in the hammock was not nearly so comfortable as the luxury of a flat mattress. We succumbed to the temptation of doing a bit of laundry. Bruce's travel books had warned that hanging up wet clothes would tempt certain flies to lay their eggs there; and the larvae (more commonly known as maggots) would then burrow into the body of the unsuspecting person who wore the clothes. We realized, however, that our towels were hung up wet every day (even our clothes "hung" wet on our sweaty bodies), so the possibility of fly larvae was just another unfortunate hazard of the African tropics.

On our last morning we were scheduled for our first sampling trip in the new sled or skimmer, Francis Hallé's innovative technique of sliding around on top of the canopy. Fortunately the dawn arrived clear and calm, conditions both essential for use of the sled. Danny got into the pilot seat and fired up the propane burner of the dirigible. Bruce, Francis, and I took our positions in separate corners of the triangular sled, and the dirigible silently lifted us into the early morning mist. The view was fabulous, with swirling wisps of low clouds interspersed among the emergent trees. Our mission was to sweep-net through the treetops in replicated fashion, utilizing the same number of sweeps for each tree. The procedure was analogous to a research boat trawling through ocean waters for plankton samples. We approached an enormous bidou tree, *Irvingia gabonensis* (family Irvingiaceae), full of purple flowers. How different it was to see this tree from above rather than from below, where its characteristic buttresses predominate and the flowers are not visible. The dirigible gently descended, enabling the sled to slide across the top of the canopy. Bruce and I "leapt" into action, each completing ten full sweeps into the foliage with our long-handled insect nets, in close proximity to our respective corners of the sled. We then inserted the net with its insect contents, into a plastic garbage bag, hastily sprayed insecticide into the opening, and sealed the bag with our catch inside. The traditional mode of analyzing the contents of a sweep net, once the replicated sweeps are completed, is patiently to extract each individual from the fabric and place it in a vial. We did not have the time or the agility on the sled to empty our nets after each set of ten sweeps. Instead, we bagged each catch still inside the net, and then used a new net to collect the next sample. Later (once we were safely back on the ground) we removed the stunned insects from each of the bags.

Our next approach into the canopy of a cardboard tree was less professional, for the sled bumped abruptly into an adjacent emergent tree. We were showered with ants, which inflicted fierce stings and bites as the dirigible hastily lifted us upward and away from further harm. Although it was difficult to negotiate the undulations in the canopy, the sled provided a new and versatile method of canopy sampling. Never before had anyone sampled relative insect abundance in replicate tree canopies in such a short time span.

After each day in the field, we would gather in the *boucarrou,* or meeting hut, for progress reports and impromptu talks about our research interests. Our last evening at camp featured a wonderful roster. We introduced Francis to the American term *ruckus,* suggesting that (figuratively) we had a ruckus of new ideas emerging from our rain-forest site. We entitled the evening seminar "Ruckus in the Rain Forest." It featured Miraculous Mycorrhizae (by Meg), Incredible Roots (by Francis), Amazing Mimicry (by Mark), and last but not least, drinks! In my talk I described my work in Australia, where we hypothesized that mycorrhizae may provide an ecological advantage to the establishment of monodominant tropical stands. Francis spoke about his architectural branch modules that are capable of rooting and establishing new units. And Mark amused everyone with his wonderful descriptions of ants and their spider mimics, including his internationally famous gyrations to imitate their antics. The fourth item on the agenda was a coveted supply of Seagram's whiskey, diplomatically shared among the audience.

As we organized our luggage prior to departure, I finally realized what had caused the continual stream of ants into my duffel bag: two lollipops (intended for my sons after my last trip to the bank in Massachusetts) were hidden in the pocket of my purse. What a mess of sugar, sticky fabric, and ants! As we were preparing to leave camp, the villagers engaged in a competition to ask (politely) for our shoes, shirts, and other articles of clothing. Since it was obvious that they needed them, we were happy to oblige.

We departed at 3:30 P.M., facing an easy drive with lighter luggage — as well as with fewer police checks, because the political situation had eased. We sensed an animated, celebratory atmosphere in Douala. Our airport exit was not entirely smooth, however: some of us had to pay the requisite bribes to get through customs or else suffer the humiliation of a body search behind a black curtain. We all gave a sigh of relief as we boarded the plane. Overnight in Paris was memorable — not because of the Eiffel Tower or the romance of the Seine, but simply because I was able to enjoy a bubble bath, a mattress, and ice in my drink.

The transition between field expeditions to the tropics and my temperate-based abode is always awkward. Those back home can never quite envision my life in the bush, nor understand what new dimensions have been added to my perspective by being temporarily without Western trappings. It took several months fully to comprehend my reentry after this trip to Cameroon — after all, I had flown across an ocean, spanned three continents, traveled between tropical and temperate zones, and — most significantly — adapted to two vastly different cultures, each with its own marvelous, but not easily interchangeable, mores and attributes.

Less than 28 percent (190,000 square kilometers as opposed to 680,000) of the original tropical rain forest remains in Western Africa, whereas as much as 55 percent (1,490,000 square kilometers of the original 2,710,000) survives in Central Africa. These levels of forest reduction are less drastic than in other parts of the world, yet the African rain forest is perhaps the most vulnerable of them all.

Only a few international conservation programs distribute funds in Africa, and there is relatively little ecotourism that could influence government policies on land use. The continent, with its unusual centers of endemism, also suffers from increasing desertification as the forests disappear.

At present I am advising a graduate student at the University of Yaounde in Cameroon who has very little opportunity to utilize computers or to access current libraries. I am also working with a botany professor there to set up epiphyte conservation programs in African villages. We are endeavoring to establish an exchange of plant materials and resources between our institutions. It is a challenge, but the future conservation of African rain forests depends primarily on the education of African students and of their governments, and we must all recognize our responsibility to the planet as a whole.

8 Construction Cranes in the Canopy

In the rain forest, no niche lies unused. No emptiness goes unfilled. No gasp of sunlight goes untrapped. In a million vest pockets, a million life-forms quietly tick. No other place on earth feels so lush. Sometimes we picture it as an echo of the original Garden of Eden — a realm ancient, serene, and fertile, where pythons slither and jaguars lope.

— Diane Ackerman, *The Rarest of the Rare,* 1995

In the 1980s, an ecologist at the Smithsonian Institution named Alan Smith pioneered a novel idea for canopy research. He suggested the use of a construction crane to access tree crowns. Although Smith's concept may have sounded preposterous ten years ago, it has revolutionized canopy research.

In 1992, after great deliberation, I left my inspiring life as a visiting professor at Williams College to become director of research and conservation at the Marie Selby Botanical Gardens in Sarasota, Florida. I knew not a soul in Florida, and even the job description was relatively vague compared to the more predictable duties of a college professor. Still, the post was compelling for many reasons. It offered direct opportunities to pursue my goal of rain-forest research and conservation. I could devote twelve months of the year to getting my feet muddy and trying to make a real difference in tropical issues, not merely discussing them in the classroom. I could engage in public education to share my convictions about conservation of natural habitats by giving firsthand accounts of my field experiences. A permanent position, it provided an element of financial security for me and the boys. And perhaps most important, Sarasota boasted an excellent public school with magnet programs in math and science (my sons' favorite subjects). Although I hoped to return to teaching someday, I wanted to devote my energies to fieldwork while I was still physically capable of climbing trees with a relative degree of safety.

I flew to Sarasota on June 30, my contract with Williams having just expired, and I began at Selby Gardens on July 1. During 1992 I experienced all the significant emotional threats that psychologists advise avoiding: divorce, moving, changing jobs, and buying a house. Although it might have been "the year from hell," surprisingly it was not — thanks to the support of family and friends. The Selby and Sarasota communities were friendly and stimulating, and the boys and I embraced a new life of activity, school, and culture. One of my first field adventures in my new position was to work on the Smithsonian's canopy crane in the seasonally dry tropical forests of Panama.

At bedtime in our house, we have a tradition called talk time. Quiet mother-son talks with each boy alone take place in the dark and cover any issue that happens to enter our heads. We have a comforting notion that darkness makes our conversations more private and anonymous than speaking in broad daylight. Regardless of the psychology, it is a very special time. Just prior to my trip to Panama, each boy said independently during his talk time that he wished he could come with me. It was the first time in my traveling career that Eddie and James had expressed any interest in getting away from the safe world of their beds, books, toys, and comforts. They were old enough now to contemplate adventure outside their own world, and they were mature enough at ages eight and six to become field assistants, not liabilities. Next time, I promised them, I would organize a family expedition.

My life had become a frenzy of research, travel, administrative, and educational duties at Selby Gardens. While I relished my office responsibilities (and even managed to squeeze in some teaching and student advising of interns at nearby New College), canopy research was suddenly becoming the "flavor of the month." Thanks to my parents' devotion to grandparenting duties, I was able to accept some of the many invitations to conduct fieldwork in different tropical forests. Ironically, as a single working parent, I was seeing more of the world than I had in any other phase of my life. I was like a child in a candy shop, for the first time, visiting places as relatively close to home as Harvard University, then going all the way to Yaounde, Cameroon, the farthest destination imaginable.

The opportunity to visit Panama and work on the canopy crane with the Smithsonian Tropical Research Institute (STRI) was a dream come true for two reasons: I was thrilled to conduct research using this amazing tool that offered the luxury of effortless transportation into the upper crowns; and I had always dreamed of seeing the Panama Canal, the incredible construction feat that had changed the course of history. I was fortunate to obtain a fellowship from the Smithsonian to work as a visiting scientist on their new canopy crane.

It was hard to believe that the relatively short distance from South Florida to Panama required a ten-hour flight. Panama City airport had a lighting system similar to that of Duoala, Cameroon: that is, none. The plane landed on a dark runway and we disembarked into a hot, muggy night. My STRI colleague was nowhere in sight. I waited nervously for fifteen long minutes, wishing desperately that I had studied Spanish rather than German in high school. A harried Joseph Wright appeared, explaining that he had driven through the dark, rainy night on a road beset with potholes, only to have a bus tire careen into his left headlight and roll off the shoulder just in front of his right bumper. "Welcome to the world of driving in Panama," he muttered.

Joe kindly took me to his home for the night, since it was too late to find my STRI apartment. He and his family lived in a sprawling house surrounded (for safety) by iron fencing. His two children, similar in age to mine, played with many of the same toys that we had in the States, but their world was very different. I lay awake for much of the night, listening to the sounds of cars and voices and eventually early-morning birds. Only a noisy air-conditioning unit can drown out the distractions of Panama City and enable visitors to sleep, I later learned. After a quick breakfast, Joe and I rushed off to experience the canopy crane.

The research site was situated in an urban forest park, Parque de Metropolitano, close to the edge of Panama City. The crane presented a curious dichotomy of man and nature. Perched on an urban hillside, it had views of incredibly large tree canopies as well as of the Panama City skyline. A sister crane off in the distance performed its more traditional role in high-rise construction. Nestled in its green oasis, the canopy crane had round-the-clock guards to protect it from vandalism. (The watchmen earned $1 per hour, the going rate in 1993.)

To reach the crane, we drove past a derelict old shed, a park entrance with gate and guard, another locked gate, then a dirt track leading to the base of the monstrous structure. The crane was permanently affixed to a cement platform, above which extended the yellow metal base that held the crane arm approximately 42 meters up into the sky. The structure was originally painted red (very photogenic), but the bright color was controversial and eventually it was repainted yellow. The difficulty of trying to predict the response of birds and wildlife, and of minimizing the invasive impact of such a large artificial structure, creates an element of risk for scientists. While cranes may not be effective in conducting studies of mammal behavior because they are potentially disruptive, they are ideal for measurements of photosynthesis—or, in my case, herbivory of foliage.

José, the crane operator, was quiet, bronzed, and strong. Deftly climbing the many metal steps to his cubicle in the sky, he could drive the gondola anywhere within the perimeter of the crane arm. José lowered a large hook to attach the gondola to the steel cable that maneuvered passengers within the tree crowns. In decided contrast to the guards, the crane driver earned $9 an hour because he possessed a technical skill that required specialized training. (The average Panamanian wage was $2 per hour.)

We stepped effortlessly into the gondola. Joe radioed his request for liftoff to José and we were airborne. What a view! Vines, orchids, goannas, more vines, tree crowns, birds, more vines, and many layers of foliage were visible in every direction. The agility of the crane was beyond belief. We hovered between trees, alighted delicately next to vines in flower, and ascended high above the crown of an *Anacardium excelsum* (family Anacardiaceae) for a photo of the sur-

Canopy construction cranes, perhaps the newest and most expensive canopy-access tools. The cranes provide complete access to every leaf within the circumference of the crane arm. I used this method in tropical dry forests in Panama to survey vines as possible pathways for insect travel. Now, a network of crane sites exists worldwide, including this one in Venezuela. Photograph by author.

face undulations of this crown. Leaves hung motionless in the early-morning stillness. Goannas lay atop the crowns, sunning themselves and oblivious to our intrusion into their private world. Insects buzzed around the epiphytes and tree flowers. The ability of the crane to reach different heights with ease and return with precision to one specific leaf was a feature that exceeded the capability of single ropes and surpassed the agility of the balloon. Even the most unfit scientist could now reach the canopy. We joked that a woman could don stiletto heels and an evening gown, serve champagne, and still conduct sampling. The crane's only obvious drawback was that access was limited to tree crowns within the radius of the crane arm.

My research project on the canopy crane was originally designed as a comparative study of the herbivory of the canopies of Panama and Australia. Joe Wright and I had proposed this project three years ago, but the funding was not forthcoming at that time, so Joe had initiated his study alone. Consequently, we used slightly different field techniques, only to find out (later) that the comparability of our data was limited. Methodology is one of the real pitfalls in field science. Sometimes the most apparently innocuous alterations of a technique can skew the data and render them impossible to compare with another data set. In this instance, Joe had expressed his herbivory in days of leaf life, while I had expressed mine as annual percentages. It was possible to correct for this temporal difference, but the time and energy required to standardize the two data sets were overwhelming.

The crane greatly facilitated my studies of herbivory in forest canopies. Leaf consumption by insects, birds, and mammals is an important process in the forest, because it represents a loss of the tissue that produces energy (via photosynthesis) for the entire forest ecosystem. Historically, the loss of leaf tissue was measured by scientists who went into a forest and simply clipped a small sample of leaves growing in the understory, returned to the laboratory with the leaves in a plastic bag, and measured their holes to calculate the portions chewed. Not surprisingly, most levels of herbivory in forests were recorded as moderate, sometimes even negligible. This method of sampling in essence ignored almost 95 percent of the foliage because it was overhead and consequently out of reach. It also "ignored" leaves that had been entirely eaten, since they were not visible to collect. With the advent of canopy-access techniques, it is now possible to measure the herbivory of the entire forest more comprehensively. Recent studies have shown that herbivory involves more than just holes in leaves. Leaf longevity, insect and bird behavior, chemistry of leaf tissue, and variation between leaves of different ages are all parts of the process in a complex forest. Perhaps most important, the phenology of the animals who eat foliage, and of the leaf flushes, must be monitored to understand herbivory. The crane made such detailed observations possible within one forest stand.

Even with a tool such as the crane, some organisms in the forest canopies remained elusive. Studying birds in tree crowns was almost impossible, owing to their relatively shy behavior. One biologist, Charles Munn, has used ultralight planes to track and observe macaws in the tropical forests of Peru. This method of study is quite dangerous, but proved successful in monitoring these important birds as they flew above the canopy. Other ornithologists have spent hundreds of hours patiently observing trees in fruit, to count and measure birds feeding. Arboreal mammals such as the bat, margay, rodent, sloth, pangolin, cuscus, orangutan, and binturong also represent challenges for biological field study. Methods for estimating populations in the treetops have not been standardized, and tropical mammalogists face enormous obstacles. Louise Emmons, a world-renowned mammalogist, has spent thousands of hours observing and trapping mammals in tropical forests, and may well make new discoveries as canopy access improves.

In Australia, galahs and other birds sometimes break off large quantities of canopy foliage, perhaps in courtship or just in playful behavior. By good fortune I happened to witness this tactic during my observations in the canopy. How significant to the tree is the impact of this intermittent behavior? How can this fatal event be accounted for in terms of leaf longevity? And how can a biologist hope to understand the impact of such an event when it may occupy only ten critical seconds in the life of a leaf?

Because Joe's herbivory project did not require my collaboration, I decided to conduct different research from the crane. I was interested in vines, and their role in deterring (or attracting) herbivores in canopies. Vines are one of the least-studied segments of canopy biology, yet they are a significant component of the forest and have been admired by naturalists for centuries. Charles Darwin wrote extensively on vines, based on his observations during his voyage on the *Beagle*. Vines depend upon tree crowns for support, yet they often restrict or even prohibit the growth of trees when they overtop the foliage. Vines have incredible modes of climbing: tendrils, twining attributes, thorns and hooks, adventitious roots, stiff leader shoots, and other strategies that render them almost mobile in their ability to exploit space in the canopy. One favorite is the Australian lawyer vine (*Calamus muelleri,* family Palmae), so named because its notorious sharp thorns hook onto skin or clothing and, like legal entanglements, never seem to let go. Jack Putz, an expert on vines, summarized their effect on forests: "Scaling to the treetops may represent success for vines but it spells doom (or at least gloom) for trees." Jack has estimated that vines constitute 25 percent of the biomass of forest on Barro Colorado Island, Panama. Many canopy vertebrates and invertebrates utilize vines for travel throughout the forest, as well as for food, shelter, escape from predators, and access to prey. Vines are common in secondary, or disturbed, forests, where they can be detrimental to forest management. Until scientists understand the abundance and function of vines in forest canopies, we cannot hope to appreciate their value to forest ecosystems.

My research question in this study was, Do vines represent pathways for herbivores in the tropical rain-forest canopy? In other words, Do vines in treetops result in higher levels of herbivory? Perhaps insects are able to travel to the treetops more frequently by virtue of the interconnectedness of the vines reaching into crowns than they can in trees without vines. To test this hypothesis, I needed to find tree canopies with vines and compare them to trees without vines. The crane was a perfect tool for this work (and the canopy raft was used to expand the study in subsequent years). From the gondola of the crane, I sampled foliage and measured herbivore damage to leaves; I also assessed populations of herbivores with a few rapid techniques (sweep nets, aspirators, and beating trays). Since this was an ecological study, I carefully sampled in exactly the same fashion and at the same time of day for each pair of trees.

After my first exhilarating day studying vines and herbivory from the canopy crane, Joe took me into town to the Tupper Building, headquarters for STRI researchers in Panama City. The building was named for the founder of Tupperware, whose donation facilitated the existence of STRI in Panama City. My intended automobile had somehow disappeared from the organization's roster, so Joe scrambled awkwardly to sort out the schedule and assured me that a vehicle would be available the next day. He kindly drove me to my apartment (with a grocery stop on the way) and provided me with a telephone number to call a taxi early the following morning. My crane time was booked from 7:00 A.M. to 11:00 A.M., hours that were rigid since other scientists required time for their projects. However, the challenge of summoning a taxi at 6:30 in the morning without a firm knowledge of geography or Spanish turned out to be overwhelming.

I awoke at 3:30 to the sound of a car crash outside my window. Evidently the driver had not noticed a large tree at the edge of the road. Much loud and angry conversation followed; sounds carried so easily through the still, humid air and the open windows of the tropics. Not knowing any Spanish expletives, I could not fully appreciate the situation. Dogs continued to bark and men were still carting away the wreckage at five o'clock, so I arose and prepared for the challenge of getting to the crane site without a reasonable command of Spanish.

I called the taxi's number and struggled to convey my message in Anglo-Spanish. The operator seemed to understand — or was he just being polite? I walked down the street to the grocery store for the presumed rendezvous with my taxi. I purchased some fruit and waited, but the cab failed to arrive. Miraculously, after a while a driver from a different taxicab company stopped to buy a drink. I eventually found a bilingual shopper, who explained my destination. The driver agreed to take me to *la Grulla*. I imagine that he found the crane a strange destination for a lone woman at that hour of the morning! He drove so fast that I never saw any of the landmarks Joe mentioned, but we quickly reached the derelict shed and the locked gate that I remembered from the day before. Mirna, Joe's assistant on his herbivory project, fortunately, was waiting.

She and I hopped into the gondola and were quickly and silently transported up into another world. It was an amazing sensation, to glide effortlessly into the treetops. Mirna and I exchanged information in our broken Spanish and English, sharing similar views about women in science, the challenges of having children with a career, and the opportunities for Mirna in Panama. How to balance family and career is truly a universal issue for women in all countries.

My hypothesis was that vines, by serving as a pathway for invertebrate travel, may lead to increased herbivory and an abundance of insects in tree crowns. I considered this sampling period on the crane a pilot study, useful to check methods and to map out a future sampling design for testing my hypothesis more extensively. In field biology, most scientists conduct pilot studies in order to determine the feasibility of a project. A great deal of time and money can be saved by trying new methods or questions on a small scale, rather than in a full-fledged field experiment.

I sampled insects in tree crowns with vines and paired them with tree crowns without vines. Only six to eight tree species dominated the canopy that was within reach of the crane, so I concentrated on them: *Anacardium excelsum* (family Anacardiaceae), *Ficus insipida* (family Moraceae), *Antirrhoea trichantha* (family Rubiaceae), *Luehea seemanii* (family Tiliaceae), *Swietenia macrophylla* (family Meliaceae), *Castilla elastica* (family Moraceae), and *Cecropia longipes* (family Cecropiaceae). These species are now famous in the ecophysiologicial literature. Teams of scientists, headed by Steve Mulkey, Kaoru Kitajima, and others, have pioneered studies on photosynthesis and leaf function from the gondola of the Panama crane. Facilitated by the crane, I conducted the sampling with ease: sweep-netting, leaf sampling for herbivory, videos, photos, and vine surveys. I counted 104 tree crowns with vines as opposed to 54 without vines. In a forest at the edge of an urban area, it is common to find signs of disturbance, including vines and secondary plant species. Eventually some vines may result in crown dieback or even mortality. But as they grow and form a network, do their sinewy stems create highways into the crowns for hungry herbivores?

Seven cranes have been funded around the world since 1992: Wind River in Washington State (evergreen coniferous forest); LeEsmeralda along the Orinoco River in Venezuela (lowland tropical rain forest); Lambir National Park, Malaysia (dipterocarp forest); Cape Tribulation, Queensland, Australia (lowland tropical rain forest); a second crane in Panama (wet tropical rain forest); a proposed site in Europe (temperate deciduous forest); and this one. The cranes have become increasingly specialized as the concept continues to expand. At Wind River, the gondola has electricity (although fraught with problems); in Venezuela, the crane moves along a tramline so that a larger number of trees are accessible; and in Malaysia, the crane is part of a major canopy-access system that will include walkways, towers, and ladders. Perhaps most encouraging of all is the fact that canopy crane researchers are beginning to collaborate and exchange information, a process that is essential to forest management and conservation on a global scale. In 1997 the International Canopy Crane Network first convened in Panama City, and ideas for future collaboration were discussed by ten scientists from around the world.

My rental vehicle was available when we returned to STRI head-quarters from the crane, so I gratefully accepted the keys and looked forward to having independent transport. As Murphy's Law would have it, the gas tank read "empty." I saw no gas station all the way home, so I said a special prayer to the GOLWITS (God-of-lone-women-in-tropical-situations) that I would have enough fuel to return to work the next day. Stopping at the grocery store near my apartment, I purchased a feast of frozen pizza, canned corn, apples, and quinine water.

I only pray to the GOLWITS on urgent occasions, I am happy to admit. Sometimes I have requested intervention regarding the weather, but most often I have simply requested safe passage in situations where a woman traveling alone may be at risk. Dressing in khaki "bush-clothes" can be misunderstood by some cultures, such as regions where the conventional garb for single women is either high heels and tight skirts, or traditional saris wrapped around the waist; I occasionally pray that villagers will accept my friendship, despite my lack of approriate dress.

In this instance the GOLWITS looked after me, and I drove back to STRI the next morning without running out of gas, and also without having to stop at a traffic light. (I had been advised to lock my doors at red lights in certain sections of Panama City.) In the elevator of the Tupper Building I met Robin Foster, whose friendship has changed my life forever. Not only did he direct me to the nearby gas station, but we ended up talking until three in the morning about shared issues of tropical plants, epiphytes, and scientific adventures.

I call Robin the missionary for the trees. His devotion to answering a huge question, "What is the most common tree in South America?" has sent him on expeditions, surveys, and quests for almost two decades. He is one of the world's authorities on tropical plants, but modest about his command of this subject. Robin invited me to accompany him to Barro Colorado Island, where I could assist his sampling, and he promised to introduce me to some of the epiphytes there. At last I would actually see the Panama Canal and travel across it by ferry to reach Barro Colorado Island.

We departed early from Panama City to reach the ferry at Gamboa, but missed it by two minutes. Through unexpected fate, I was able to spend a day at the Summit Botanical Gardens located on the road between Panama City and Gamboa. Robin gave me a crash course on the trees of Panama, and we watched oropendolas fly in and out of their communal nesting "villages," each with a beautiful pendulous nest hanging down like a large version of the nest of the Baltimore oriole (my temperate bias at work again). The oropendolas are probably my favorite tropical bird. Diane Ackerman aptly describes their voice as " a wet, two-stage warble, a liquid undulating smooch, part throb, part Moog synthesizer, [that] ends with the sound of a debutante throwing kisses underwater." They have an amazing lifestyle in addition to their communal canopy nesting. For one thing, they like to share their treetop nesting sites with hornets. Why hornets? The hornets kill botflies, which parasitize the baby oropendolas if left unchecked. To make the ecology of oropendolas even more complex, they also allow cowbirds to lay eggs in their nests — because the baby cowbirds are another predator on botflies.

Botflies parasitize humans as well, and no tropical biologist has earned his or her salt without an intriguing botfly story. These insects lay their eggs underneath the skin, and the fly larva hatches, grows, and fidgets within its human cavity, often tickling or irritating its human repository. As the larva grows larger, it produces a snorkel that provides an air spout to the surface. Although eventually the larva will emerge from its human home under the skin, many people find it impossible to endure the several months of gestation and lure the larva out with devious means. A piece of raw meat placed on top of the snorkel is evidently adequate bait to entice a botfly larvae to move, and tales of other unique decoys have been passed down through field station legends.

As Robin and I stopped to watch a large ship pass through the canal, one of my lifelong dreams was fulfilled. The Panama Canal was dwarfed by an Asian freighter, and I was awed to think of the many thousands of miles of sea travel that were avoided with this engineering feat. At 8:00 P.M. we arrived at Barro Colorado Island (BCI), having made the afternoon ferry with minutes to spare. (Robin told me later that he never likes to arrive at airports or boats with more than a few minutes to spare, so evidently his just-missing the earlier ferry was not unusual.) I was assigned a room in the old Chapman Building, above some of the laboratory space, and I fell asleep to the noises of unidentified Orthoptera and tree frogs.

I awoke to the unmistakable moans and growls of howler monkeys outside my window, a sound that remains one of the most vivid in my lifelong-list of unique noises. There were also many human sounds, as the BCI staff prepared for a big day celebrating the seventieth birthday of STRI. People cooked and made decorations and swept paths and hallways despite the constant traipsing of scientists with their muddy boots. At 2:00 P.M. there were speeches, dancing by a Panamanian troupe, and delicious food. That evening I was invited for drinks with Egbert Leigh, one of the island's premier scientists. The legendary Bert is a brilliant biologist who can expound on almost any scientific topic and is very endearing in his mannerisms, including his predilection to drink scotch with visiting scientists. When he first met me, he said, "It is nice to meet you, Meg-mono-dominant-forest-Lowman; I enjoyed your paper in *American Naturalist,* 1987, volume 134, pages 88–119." He seems to possess a photographic memory for everything he reads, a wonderful attribute for a scientist working in a relatively remote place. We discussed monodominant stands, photosynthesis, and other issues, and I consider myself lucky to have heard his ideas.

The next day I dashed off with Joe Wright, Robin, and the Gunatellekes, who are Sri Lankan biologists, to see Joe's seedling plots, reputedly similar to our transects in Australia. In absentminded scientific fashion, we dawdled and talked along the trail until we actually ran out of time to get to the plots. We had to turn back hastily in order to make the return ferry. In typical Robin Foster style, we dashed onto the bow of the boat just as it was backing out of the dock. I arrived in Panama City, had dinner with new friends from three countries, and prepared for my dawn flight back to the United States.

My perceptions of canopy research had been changed forever. With the ongoing collaboration of scientists and their funds, the canopy crane can offer unprecedented access to individual tree crowns. This method has facilitated intensive studies of the leaves and growth processes of tree crowns. Research on photosynthesis and gas exchange, contours of canopy surfaces and their effects on microclimate, and new topics such as canopy ants sequestering nitrogen from cockroaches or epiphytes housing earthworms in their rosette bases can be carried out with great accuracy. My pilot studies revealed that trees with vines had significantly higher levels of herbivory than trees without vines, but I need to undertake several more years of more extensive sampling to confirm this preliminary finding. Thanks to the efforts of STRI, tropical research has advanced from the forest floor into the canopy.

9 Our Treehouse in Belize

D eep in Belize, in Central America, there is a place called Blue Creek. In this shadowed world, pierced occasionally by slivers of sunlight, are more varieties of living things than perhaps any other place on earth. . . . Viewed from an airplane, the rainforest at Blue Creek looks like a field of gigantic broccoli. . . . At Blue Creek a canopy walkway designed by specialists in rainforest platform construction has been built.

— Kathryn Lasky, *The Most Beautiful Roof in the World,* 1997

As part of my role as public educator in a botanical garden, I was honored to serve as a scientist-mentor for a program called the Jason Project for Education. Jason was conceived by Dr. Robert Ballard, who discovered the Titanic *on the ocean floor and realized that it was difficult to "share" scientific discoveries in remote places with young students. He designed an education program whereby film crews go to remote locations with scientists, produce live broadcasts via satellite transmission centers, and relay them to schools, museums, and other education centers. In its fifth year Jason in 1994 explored the rain-forest canopy of Belize. I was a chief scientist, and my investigations of plant-insect relationships in the tree crowns were shared via telecommunication with hundreds of thousands of students in the United States, Canada, Central America, the United Kingdom, and Bermuda. It was nerve-racking to walk along narrow, swaying canopy bridges while talking to a camera, but I miraculously managed to keep my balance throughout all fifty-one live broadcasts.*

My children and I boarded a small six-seater plane with a simple propeller engine. Along its side the words *Maya Airways* were almost worn off. Our luggage was thrown casually into the back, and Eddie was invited to serve as copilot. He donned a pair of heavy headphones and we were off into the skies over Belize. I felt somewhat apprehensive about putting my precious children on this old propeller plane, but there was no other mode of transport to our field site. (Four years later both pilot and plane crashed into the Maya Mountains.)

My young sons were thrilled to be accompanying their mom on a tropical rain-forest expedition. Eddie was eight years old, James was six. (They had seen the Australian rain forest on numerous occasions as infants, but were too young then to remember any details.) Our destination was Blue Creek in southern Belize. Our mission was to set up the study site for the Jason Project, including the construction of a canopy walkway with several platforms upon which to conduct field research. I called this structure my green laboratory, but the boys called it their giant treehouse.

We flew for almost an hour, passing over mangrove coastline, with muddy rivers emptying into the ocean. The recent rains had caused erosion of the topsoil upstream, and it had formed bands of muddy necklaces where the estuaries met the sea. Soil erosion is a severe loss in tropical areas, where agricultural clearing exposes the soils to heavy rains. In contrast, the original forests, with their dense root mats, conserve both the soil and the runoff moisture. We saw many small, steep hillsides of rain forest dotted with milpas (cleared areas for growing corn, squash, or other small crops). The geology in southern Belize is called karst topography — tiny mountains interspersed with valleys underlain with limestone bedrock.

This was my second journey to the rain forests of Belize. Upon arriving at the Punta Gorda airport (one dirt runway and a small shack for shelter during rain or hot sun) we were met by an old truck with some of the Jason Project crew. We clambered into the truck bed and bumped along from the coastal town of Punta Gorda about 20 miles west, into the interior. At Blue Creek village Eddie and James caused quite a commotion among the village children. The arrival of two towheads — probably almost of marriage age in their culture — aroused great curiosity. The girls brought samples of their bracelets and embroidery to show the boys. James (still in his antigirl stage) was horrified; Eddie (slightly older) was friendly, but did not know how to handle such lavish attention. They passed shyly into the forest, traipsing down the new trail built to access the canopy research station, future site of our giant treehouse.

This was the first year that the Jason Project had ventured into Central America, and the first time that a terrestrial ecosystem was being emphasized. Traditionally, Jason was limited to marine research. The underlying theme of this year's program was to follow a raindrop down through the rain-forest canopy of Belize, into a cave, and offshore onto the coral reefs. I was selected to be the canopy scientist, and my colleague for the ocean was Jerry Wellington, a coral reef biologist from the University of Houston, Texas. (Typical of the interconnectedness of scientists, I had met Jerry fifteen years ago when he was a graduate student at the University of California in Santa Barbara and I was a visiting researcher.) During the Jason broadcasts, Jerry and I were instructed to conduct field research and to talk to students at the various Primary Interactive Network (PIN) sites, who would ask questions about science, scientists, and conservation. The project was an excellent opportunity to combine the missions of education, research, and conservation.

Bob Ballard and Jerry and I had traveled to Belize on the first reconnaissance trip in May 1993 with a diverse team of experts: Bob's assistant, who organized his busy life with high efficiency; a public relations agent, who managed to phone home frequently and hear messages on her answering machine (I did not even own an answering machine at this time, much less know how to access it from the jungles of Belize, and portable telephones were not yet available); an educator working on the Jason curriculum, who was warmly enthusiastic as she experienced the rain forest for her first time; a logistics officer, who was everywhere at once yet managed to do everything well; an engineer from Electronic Data Systems (EDS), the sponsor of the satellite telecommunication setup; a cameraman, who recorded our activities; and another EDS representative, who managed to look fabulous every day, including color-coordinated lipstick and color-coordinated handbag with each outfit.

We had met a wonderful diversity of scientists scattered throughout Belize, all working independently on interesting projects: Bruce and Carolyn Miller, who were expert naturalists specializing in canopy birds; Tineke and Ian Meerman, who studied Odonata (dragonflies) and herpetology (snakes and reptiles), respectively; Sharon Mattola, a field biologist and founder of the Belize Zoo; Jim and Marguerite Bevis, ecotourism operators who were proponents of environmental education in Belize; and Jeff Corwin, our expedition outfitter.

In northern Belize we had explored several locations, looking for the perfect Jason treehouse site. I wanted a diverse array of trees, with trunks large enough to support a canopy walkway; Bob Ballard wanted a spot that was picturesque and appropriate for filming; the logistics officers wanted a site where food, housing, and technical equipment would be accessible; the engineers wanted to have enough open space to park a satellite dish; and Jerry Wellington simply wanted to get to the reef. We rode a bus driven by Crazy Eddie of the Batty Bus Company (it almost sounded like a comic strip) and stopped at numerous sites in central Belize. We hiked through the valleys behind the Mountain Equestrian Lodge and heard the rare keel-billed motmot calling. We visited the Belize Zoo and observed tapirs, puma, coatamundi, and toucans. We slept at Pine Mountain Resort and woke to the sweet smell of pine trees. We passed through burned-out hillsides, where Mennonite settlements had innocently cleared the precious forest in order to create grazing lands. We drove to the coastal town of Dangriga and endured a night at the ghastly Jungle Huts (a misnomer because there was no jungle in sight). In southern Belize we traveled through Punta Gorda along an extremely bumpy dirt road to the small village of Blue Creek. After many days of searching for the perfect site, it was there that our ideas would become a reality.

Blue Creek was a leased preserve, operated by a small ecotourism venture back in Boston. The site offered little except an outhouse and one shed that served as kitchen, library, dining room, and sleeping area. But it had a superb tract of primary forest and a captivating limestone cave just 500 meters upstream from the "lodge." Across the creek were several magnificent and photogenic trees, including a bobo tree (*Pachira aquatica,* family Bombacaceae) festooned with epiphytes, aroids (*Philodendron* sp., family Araceae) with their hanging roots and small orchids clinging to the upper branches, several large epiphytes (*Aechmea* sp., family Bromeliaceae) with their tank-like rosettes holding numerous unknown and possibly new species of invertebrates, several vines of the family Bignoniaceae, and all sorts of undiscovered biodiversity. Although Belize was a country new to me, I found familiar botanical friends — coffee bush, legumes, and many plants similar to those in Panama.

We had reservations to stay at the Blue Creek "lodge" that night. Accommodations included the opportunity to lay out a sleeping bag on the floor of the open hut, or (in my fortunate situation) to tie a hammock between two posts. I had brought my faithful khaki hammock from the jungles of Cameroon, and the rest of the group was impressed. Everyone was in bed by 7:00 P.M. because there was no electricity and it was pouring rain. Sleeping in the rain forest was a new experience for most of our group. Several of the neophytes expressed concern about the risk of snakes while sleeping on the floor, and others looked about anxiously for bats. Only minutes after everyone had finally settled into his or her sleeping bag, we all leapt up at the sound of a loud explosion. A large fruit from the overhanging bobo tree (similar in size to the cannonball tree, named for the obvious size and shape of its fruits) had fallen on the tin roof. Its fruits were slightly larger than coconuts, and weighed more. Everyone laughed nervously and settled back down for a relatively sleepless night. I had often wondered why a coconut or a cannonball fruit had never killed an unsuspecting human in the understory; its plummeting descent certainly generated enough impact to fatally dent even the most hardheaded scientist. Yet I have never heard of this as a cause of mortality.

The onslaught of bobo fruits continued intermittently all night, and each time one hit our tin roof, a leak broke through. I felt strong nostalgia for my expedition to Cameroon. Not only was I sleeping in the same hammock, which still smelled like Africa, but I also experienced equal success with my bladder — twelve hours without a trip to the outhouse. Like Cameroon, Belize had army ants that foraged the forest floor in great gangs at night; fortunately, I did not trample any of them and suffer the painful bites that I did in Africa.

Our outfitter, Jeff, and another member of our group decided to explore the village of Blue Creek that night. Because of the torrential rain, they spent the night on the floor of a Belizean hut. The night noises that they experienced in the village were evidently much more unusual than ours, including pigs fornicating on the floor, children whimpering with malaria, and chickens clucking in their ears.

After that first night in the Belizean jungle, we awoke to a glistening green world. Each leaf was dripping water from the evening storms, and every drip tip was functioning to funnel water off the leaf surface and onto the root system. I mapped trees at this site, examined the canopies with binoculars to estimate epiphyte diversity, and brainstormed with the crew about possible camera angles. We traveled back to Punta Gorda in the evening, slept in real beds, and absorbed the sounds of a tropical town — bicycles pedaling on bumpy streets, skinny dogs barking, frogs peeping, music and voices emanating from tiny open-air drinking huts, and a gentle drizzle cooling the sultry summer air.

I returned the next day to Belize City, and on to Miami and Sarasota. My brain was reeling with enthusiasm and ideas. The next few months were chockablock full with planning for design and budget of the walkways, assembly of expert arborists to build the giant treehouse, writing the curriculum, answering questions from teachers and reporters, and, most important, thinking about the critical messages that I wanted to convey to students during my broadcast time. Several themes raced through my mind: deforestation, biodiversity, the challenges of ecological sampling, the intricate plant-animal relationships in the canopy, nutrient cycling, and the health of global ecosystems.

Three months flew by. By the time they were over, my walkway partner, Bart Bouricius, and I had designed and created a budget for our green laboratory. We had assembled a team of six experts for the erection of the walkway. Huts had been built that more than quadrupled the space of the field station, and foam mattresses and bunk-bed frames were flown in at great expense. Earlier, Robin Foster and I had visited Blue Creek to map and identify all the plants in the area. We spent many late-night hours pressing specimens between newspapers and recording notes about the site. Robin, a well-traveled expert on tropical plants, was extremely impressed with the diversity of Blue Creek, so it looked as if Jason had selected a site of extensive scientific interest for its broadcasts.

When my sons and I had settled into our camp site at the Blue Creek research station, we eagerly looked around us. The research station had changed dramatically since I had been there several weeks ago with Robin. Spanning the Blue Creek watercourse hung a stainless steel cable, and on either side a wooden platform had been built about 75 feet from the ground. Using our binoculars, we could observe the arborists, like a troupe of monkeys, "performing" overhead. The conversations were unbelievable: "Can you lower the bosun's chair?" " I need an 18-inch eye-bolt up here" "Does anyone have a pear-shaped sling link?" "Don't stand underneath me; these bolt clippers might fall." Meanwhile, the botanists had their own language that was predominant at ground level: "Here's a Rubiaceae." "Wow, check out this Lecythidaceae." "Hmmmm . . . Pterocarpus again." After many months of planning, the canopy walkway was taking shape.

My sons Eddie (*left*) and James (*right*), in Belize, preparing for their first climb. Using new harnesses they had received for Christmas, they collected insects for a school science project on canopy bio-diversity. Despite the innova-tive nature of their project, they did not win a prize. Photograph by Christopher Knight.

Eddie and James were eager to climb. They had been given chil-dren's harnesses for Christmas, so each had his own canopy gear. We had practiced at home, but this was the big time. Ironically, I was very anxious and not looking forward to having them ascend 75 feet into the sky. Even though I did this sort of thing virtually every day, it seemed more dangerous when I contemplated the ascent for my children. I knew, however, that they were probably more agile than I! My brother Ed, an expert woodworker who had helped build the platforms, was part of the construction crew. He was the "dirt" of our walkway crew (the person member who works at ground level). Ed generously offered to accompany the boys to the top and promised to call me when they were on the bridge (so that I could open my eyes). In no time the three of them had ascended the lad-

The canopy at last! My children were assisted in their first canopy climb by my brother (Ed Lowman, *sitting at right*) and an undergraduate student from New College whom I was advising (Kelly Keefe, *standing*). Here we are, enjoying the view from 75 feet in the treetops of Belize. Photograph by author.

der that hugged the *Pterocarpus* sp. (family Leguminosae) and reached the platform overlooking the creek. I hastily climbed up to join the jubilant crew.

Eddie and James were ecstatic. They saw epiphytes and watched a hummingbird sip nectar from a bromeliad. Several ant gardens decorated the bullet tree (*Terminalia amazonica,* family Combretaceae) supporting one of the research platforms. Ant gardens are an amazing phenomena to us temperate folks. They are conglomerates of canopy plants whose seeds have been carefully harvested and carted by the ants to a central site. The ants nurture and tend their garden, creating a diverse miniature system in the treetops that can include cactuses, Peperomia, bromeliads, orchids, and occasional vines. The ants gain shelter and food, and the plants gain protection. The system is a classic example of symbiosis, in that both partners benefit from the relationship.

A look at the tranquil stream below gave us a vivid respect for our height. The people at ground level looked like ants. We saw the glistening sun leaves and felt the winds gusting over the emergent flame tree (*Bernoullia flammea,* family Bombacaceae) adjacent to our platform. The flame tree had lost half its leaves and would probably be bare by late March. It was one of the few deciduous species in this tropical evergreen-dominated rain forest. Although most people assume that all tropical trees have evergreen leaves, this is not the case. Some are deciduous on a regular basis, and some are partially deciduous depending on the advent of a dry season. The flame tree will flower before producing a new flush of leaves; its array of pinkish-red blooms provides a stunning flame of color in the sea of green canopy trees.

The canopy was a whole new world for Eddie and James, and a whole new world for me to appreciate through their eyes. They cautiously crossed the bridge over the creek, which spanned approxi-

Leaves of the flame tree (*Bernoullia flammea*). Our treetop research lab in Belize was situated in the crown of the tree. Deciduous, it shed its leaves in March; just before leafing again, the entire tree became pink with flowers. Illustration by Barbara Harrison.

One of the canopy walkways that provide safe and permanent access to many tree crowns. My children on the canopy walkway built in Belize for the Jason Project, demonstrate the ease of mobility. Photograph by Ed Lowman.

mately 72 feet and had a well-defined sway in the center. Once on the other side, they peered in awe at the white poisonwood tree (*Sebastiana* sp., family Euphorbiaceae), whose leaves reputedly inflict an irritating rash to human skin if touched.

After several exploratory hours in the canopy, the boys descended on the metal staples and ladders to the ground below. With elation they observed a hairy black tarantula on the tree trunk. It looked identical to our faithful pet spider, Harriet, at home. The day was a huge success. The boys did not even seem to mind their dinner of beans and rice, despite the fact that it was the fourth night of that menu.

As I might have guessed, my children had no trouble adapting to arboreal life. Will they become scientists like their mother? At this

James (*left*) and Eddie (*right*), assisting their mom with insect sampling during the Jason Project. They are using a beating tray in the canopy of Belize. Another undergraduate student whom I was advising (David Scholle from Williams College) is watching as I take notes on the catch. Photograph by Christopher Knight.

point in their lives, their answer is an enthusiastic Yes, but the many years ahead may corrupt those young intentions.

We decided to take a night walk, because many insects in the rain forest, especially herbivores that munch on foliage, are more active at night than during the day. In my Australian fieldwork the rain forest had been noisy at night owing to the prevalent chewing of walking sticks and beetles during times of new leaf flush. Would the situation be similar in Belize? We donned our head lamps and our wet sneakers. After the first day in Belize, everything we owned was either soaking wet from the heavy rains or extremely soggy from the humidity. (For ten days I could hardly write in my notebooks because of the high humidity; for subsequent stays at Blue Creek I brought back waterproof notebooks.) Several hundred feet down the trail James spotted a glistening spiderweb that seemed to be shaking. It was a windless night, so we were curious. Was the spider engaged in battle? Was it wrestling with some giant prey? We looked closely. The orb was beautiful and neat, with a long thread pulled through its middle. As we stood watching, suddenly this thread snapped and the entire web released like a rubber band. We jumped back in surprise, and the boys said in unison, "A slingshot spider." A new species was defined (or so we surmised). We watched this slingshot action several times. The spider actually pulled back its central thread and then released it when an unsuspecting prey flew past. Several other slingshot spiders were in the vicinity, so I carefully collected one in a vial to return to the Smithsonian for identification. What a novel variation on the traditional spiderweb capture mechanism!

On our return to camp we watched masses of army ants swarm around the perimeter, and we were grateful for the stilts beneath our cabin. The ants ran on top of one another in a frenzied dash along some highway whose edges were probably marked by a special ant pheromone, their destination unknown except to the ants in the forward section of the group. When we got to our bunks, Eddie noticed a strange black shape on the rafter above his head. A tarantula had decided to come in out of the rain and take shelter on our ceiling. We all decided that Eddie would never sleep with this apparition several feet above his head. So I gently prodded it with a broom until it fell to the floor, then escorted it out the front door, where it could roost on the verandah instead.

On our last day, the boys counted fourteen rain showers. We were ready to go home. My sons, bedraggled in their muddy attire, considered themselves fortunate to have shared this pristine rain forest with its residents. Sadly, many children will grow up without ever being bathed in tropical mud or immersed in jungle adventures. And if the current levels of rain-forest destruction continue, such privileges will no longer be possible.

I returned to Blue Creek the following month, to begin broadcasting the Jason Project from our green laboratory. There was a large EDS truck with a satellite dish 15 feet in diameter parked at the edge of our woodland trail into Blue Creek. The Mayans were gathered around a large television screen watching the Olympics. Three wires were strung a half-mile into the camp, and guards discreetly kept watch over the paraphernalia. The camp was a chaotic contrast of new and old. Large metal boxes containing computers and sound apparatus and electronic equipment lay on tarps underneath the rain-forest canopy, and Mayans walked quietly in their bare feet with tumplines across their foreheads to haul the equipment into the forest. Our scientific agenda seemed an inconsequential third or fourth rank in importance. The walkway, however, looked enticing and I was eager to get up there and escape the chaos on the ground.

A distinguished visitor came to camp on our first day in residence. The Duke of Edinburgh was arriving by helicopter to visit the Jason Project and experience his first lesson in canopy biology. Promptly at noon a group of bodyguards strutted into camp, surrounding a thin, gaunt gentleman dressed casually in a light blue safari shirt with white buttons. Everyone was introduced, and one of the Jason crew nearly got manhandled when he tried to take a photo without official permission. Prince Philip was charming — and extremely interested in our green laboratory in the treetops. Although he was not allowed to climb for obvius reasons of safety and security, I pointed out all the sections of our giant treehouse and summarized the ongoing research. He walked nimbly along the forest track, navigating rocks and slippery sections with apparent ease. At lunch I sat on his right and Bob Ballard on his left. (At that moment it was hard to believe that five years ago I had been washing dishes and picking up Lego in my kitchen in outback Australia.) The duke discussed many issues with our scientific team; clearly, he felt a great sense of urgency about world population growth and tropical forest conservation. He kindly agreed to let me organize a photo of the two of us, to give my children, then departed after lunch in a helicopter. Its blades were kept just above the upper canopy to minimize leaf loss from downdrafts. The royal visit had been a success, and now we could turn our thoughts to science via satellite. I jumped into the Blue Creek, and while the fish nipped my extremities I floated in the current, thinking about field biology and watching a hummingbird speed into its nest just outside the cabin where Eddie and James had stayed with me only one month ago.

Our last night prior to our final rehearsal was marked by a tremendous downpour. We raced to the cameras and microscopes, covering fragile items just in time. The Jason crew was full of talent: Carl, the assistant producer; Gordie, a tall and funny man who would stalk Bob Ballard by camera; Bob, the cameraman assigned to me because he was exactly my height; Shari and Michael, the producers who had just become engaged; Jackson, the fast-paced grip (he not only rigged the sets, but climbed in and around the platforms); Tom Miller, a speleologist (cave geologist); his assistant, John, from England; Jorge, who was coordinating the Blue Creek villagers; a team of students and teachers as research assistants; and of course Bob Ballard. Roughly forty people were working as a team to produce Jason from the remote rain forest of Belize. After dinner we joined the Mayan village to watch the Olympics on the large-screen EDS television. I returned to my tent to find the bed soaking wet; numerous leaks had sprung in my tarp during the downpour.

I had the honor of giving the Duke of Edinburgh his first exposure to forest canopies at our "treehouse" in Belize. Photograph by Nate Erwin.

Our first broadcast was scheduled for 9:00 A.M. on Monday, February 28. I woke at three o'clock to hear an ominous wind blowing, the first time I had ever heard leaves rustle in this valley. Was it an omen of poor weather? As we rushed through breakfast (beans and rice, of course) and prepared for our stations, Carl suffered a bad electric shock on the main platform when he turned on a TV monitor. Miraculously, the short was quickly pinpointed to a wire that was spanning the creek underwater. It was hastily repaired. The day became sunnier, although the weather never quite behaved according to plan.

All of the "actors" had earphones connected remotely to the studio hut, so I could hear the countdown. Suddenly we were on the air. Bob Ballard smiled and said, "Hi, I'm Bob Ballard . . ." as he walked jauntily across the long walkway to my research platform. It was exciting; things went well. The Jason students were a great success, and my ride down in the bosun's chair to vertically tour the canopy layers was exhilarating. The promised hour off for each scientist never materialized, so I was grateful when it was four o'clock and I could take a well-deserved swim. Clambering around the walkways in front of the camera was a hot and sticky proposition, especially at 90°F with high humidity.

By the second day of broadcasting, we had worked out a few more bugs (no pun intended). The chef served sticky buns for breakfast, my favorite. The food during the Jason broadcast was miraculous; after beans and rice every day in January, we were now eating gourmet jungle fare. It consisted of a lot of tough chicken, as well as good old beans and rice, but also many imported goodies including apple pie, to satisfy this New York–based film crew. An enormous chunk of ice was even brought in to keep the Belizean beer cold.

On March 4 I wished my mother happy birthday on air. Canopy research had come a long way since my initial climb on this date in 1979. The members of the production crew were fascinating, and between broadcasts we sat in the tree canopies all day sharing our stories and philosophies of life. Oddly, I began to know more about these new friends than about many of those back home. Often, people seem to bare their souls in remote locales.

My assistant scientist for this project was Nathan Erwin, director of the Insect Zoo at the Smithsonian Institution. Nate and I have been friends since we were twelve, when I first taught him how to make an insect-collecting net at a summer camp. I am proud that he has gone on to direct the foremost entomological exhibit in America. Nate collected insects from the canopy during the Jason broadcasts, while I measured herbivory and other interactions.

The students enjoyed the gadgets used for sampling insects in the canopy. We had a traditional insect net, which captured flying insects very effectively. We also used beating trays — 3′ × 3′ cloth trays that accumulated insects when the foliage overhead was vigorously shaken. Beating trays were most effective for capturing insects that rested on leaf surfaces. Perhaps the most creative tool for insect capture was the aspirator (also called a pooter because of the sound it makes). It consisted of two rubber tubes attached to a vial; the user sucked an insect into the vial. The clever design featured a mesh between the vial and the tubing that was placed into the sampler's mouth, thereby preventing any insects from being inhaled. In addition, we used a Malaise trap that consisted of gauze walls shaped to encourage insects to fly in, but not out. Used together, these techniques gave a better estimate of the biodiversity in a site than using one method alone.

One day on air, I measured the leaf area of a cohune palm (*Orbignya cohune,* family Palmae), also called a testicle palm because of the unique pendant form of its paired fruits. The leaf surface of one frond measured 6.1 square meters, which established a record in my sampling experience as the largest leaf. During another broadcast the Duke of Edinburgh returned to "visit" us from Bermuda via telecommunication. I offered commentary while he drove our remote-operated camera through the canopy. We used a remote camera that traveled on its own track and relayed images of the canopy back to our base camp, as well as to sites throughout North America to which we were linked via satellite.

Each day we adopted a theme for the six hour-long shows. Topics included the use of tools in research, scientific hypotheses, and the continuum of research (in the sense of passing ideas on to the next generation).

After five days of broadcasting, the "talent" (the nickname for those who starred in the broadcasts) were invited to spend a night in town. I had grown rather accustomed to my leaky tent, but the thought of a hot shower, flush toilet, and real bed was tempting. Punta Gorda was almost an hour away on bumpy dirt roads, yet only 20 miles on the map. Once there we slept in air-conditioned rooms, and I certainly appreciated the white noise instead of voices through the night as the film crew tinkered and adjusted their equipment. In all justice, though, setting up a film studio in a rough jungle was an unimaginable task. I learned a lot of new vocabulary: L-cut, voice-over, IFB, roll-in, canopy cam, and boom.

Our walkway in Belize was a scientist's dream. We had five platforms, ranging in height from 75 feet to 125 feet (the crow's nest). Platforms were connected by a series of bridges and ladders. The trees ranged from the hardwood evergreen bullet tree (*Terminalia amazonica,* family Combretaceae) to the deciduous flame tree (*Bernoullia flammea,* family Bombacaceae). We had ant gardens, parasitic plants, incredible katydids, scorpions, tarantulas, and many UFOs (unidentified flying objects). I spent one night sleeping in the canopy, since many students asked what it would be like. It was magical. I was elated to be up there in the dark and savor the symphony of insect voices.

Argonauts (student assistants) participated in our research, and teachers were also on site. I established a lasting friendship with D. C. Randle, the Jason teacher from Minnesota. It was apparent from his rapport with the students that D. C. was a brilliant teacher — and a wonderful mentor for African-American students. He teased me constantly about the fact that I would never mention the local name for the cohune palm (the aforementioned testicle palm) on the air. When he returned to Minnesota after his week of residence at Blue Creek, he cajoled one of his students into asking me (with hundreds of thousands of ears listening) "Dr. Lowman, what is the *other* name for the cohune palm?" I was forced to reply, and hundreds of thousands of students broke into gales of laughter!

One night Tom Miller, the speleologist, invited a group of us terrestrial workers to visit his cave. Tom had been mapping and exploring caves in Belize for ten years and more. We donned helmets and headlamps, and walked reverently into a different world. The cave had several pools and a few ladder descents, but otherwise was very navigable. Owing to the intense heat and humidity, I paused near a pool and told the rest of the group to continue along. They turned a corner and suddenly I was alone in the dark. It was not only dark but totally silent. What a privilege to sit in a completely dark and silent space on our planet! I heard a tiny scuttle and turned on my headlamp just in time to observe an albino whip scorpion. Sitting still had its rewards; this was the very creature that our group had hoped to see. Nearby was a provision tree seedling. This large fruit had drifted into the cave and germinated in the rocks. It too was albino, with no green tissue at all. It had absolutely no hope of survival here, but I admired its perseverance.

On our the last night together, the film crew presented us with a gift: a humorous video of our "boo-boos" set to rock music. The party later degenerated into a jungle disco, and — like proud parents — Bob Ballard and I led off the dancing with an exhibition tango. The celebration continued into the wee hours. Despite the state-of-the-art sound system, I found it impossible not to glance up occasionally at the tall trees against the vast array of stars, and appreciate that I was in the midst of a tropical rain forest.

The opportunity to share a chapter of life with these talented people had been special indeed. The nonscientists had learned about rain forests, and we scientists had learned about cameras and electronics. Beyond that, the teamwork had been wonderful, and sharing the rain forest with thousands of students had been achieved thanks to the incredible technology of the Jason Project.

10 Canopy Research from the Bottom Up

A gallery filled with the choicest paintings may soon become monotonous to one without knowledge of its history; and the halls of a great museum, so full of interest to one versed in the subjects they display, quickly become tedious to the mere wonder seeker. The fascination of the forest grows along with our foundation of knowledge and our skill in uncovering its well guarded secrets.

— Alexander Skutch, *A Naturalist in Costa Rica,* 1971

*My attempts to study canopy life have come full circle, from ground-based ob-
servations to advanced technology and back to simple tools. For in May 1995
I commenced an exciting canopy survey, yet the principal mode of canopy access was binoculars!*

*Robin Foster and I, sharing an interest in tropical trees, decided to exam-
ine the crown status of trees on Barro Colorado Island, site of a 50-hectare plot
that has captured the interest of biologists worldwide. This project had evolved
from conversations during our previous visit to BCI in 1993. Ironically, despite many intensive studies of the trees on this plot, no one had examined their
dynamics above a height of 2 meters. With my interest in epiphytes and canopy
biology, and Robin's interest in phenology and his intimate knowledge of this
plot, we elected to survey the crowns of all large trees in the parcel.*

The 50-hectare plot (as it is commonly called) on Barro Colorado
Island provides a unique opportunity for biologists to work in a
tropical rain forest in a true collaborative spirit. A large database of
information on the plot exists, and for someone such as myself who
has worked for years in remote solo situations, it was gratifying to
find information on many aspects of plant demography and life his-
tories for this site.

The plot is situated on an island of 1,500 hectares in the middle of
Gatun Lake, Panama, that was formed after flooding between 1911 and
1914 during the construction of the Panama Canal. It is a semiever-
green, seasonal forest (termed *tropical moist forest* by the Holdridge
Life-Zone system) with approximately 2,500 millimeters of rainfall
annually. During the dry season of December to April many, but certainly not all, of the trees flush new leaves and also undergo bursts
of flowering and fruiting.

In the late 1970s Robin Foster and Stephen Hubbell decided to
study the demography of tropical trees and to make observations of
the stability of tree populations over time, in the hope of explaining
the dynamics of species richness of tropical rain forests. To conduct

Binoculars — the most simple method for collecting information about the canopy. Sometimes ineffective, they are not accurate for surveying insects, but they were useful here to identify epiphytes in the crowns of trees on Barro Colorado Island, Panama. Robin Foster and I are getting stiff necks as we gaze into the crown of a tall *Ceiba pentandra* (great kapok tree). Photograph by author.

their fieldwork, they mapped and measured over 250,000 trees and saplings greater than 1 centimeter in diameter. Each stem was tagged, measured, identified, and mapped. It was an enormous amount of information to record, and certainly a daunting amount of time was spent both in the field and in front of the computer. At last count Robin had reported roughly three hundred species of trees within the plot. The data collected there have changed our way of thinking about tropical forests and promoted long-term research as a most effective scientific tool.

I felt privileged to tread this hallowed ground, whose purpose was similar to that of Joe Connell's and my long-term sites in Australia. Robin's plot was designed twenty years after Joe's parcels were first measured, but it is larger and more regular in dimension, utilizing a design that is reproducible in other tropical forests.

It is hard to conceive the tedious hours required to map, mark, and identify all the trees in 50 hectares of forest. Robin modestly told funny stories about traipsing around this plot for months with teams of assistants to survey and census all the stems. One of the commonest shrubs, *Hybanthus* sp. (family Violaceae), numbered over 250,000 individuals. Today this enormous database has generated a plethora of ecological studies on the competition, pathogens, growth, mortality, phenology, and reproduction of tropical trees.

Only binoculars, notebooks, and pencils were required to conduct our canopy study—plus an eye for vines, crown health, and epiphytes. Strong neck muscles were an asset. It was a new challenge for me as a canopy specialist to document accurately what I saw overhead while I was standing on the ground. Like the early naturalists who first entered tropical rain forests, I experienced a certain frustration in being a terrestrial creature, unable to climb easily and examine life in the treetops. I felt akin to those pioneer explorers who first observed the canopy from below and speculated (sometimes wrongly) about the complex array above.

A passage from the German explorer Alexander von Humboldt comes to mind. Recalling a visit to the rain forest in Venezuela more than one hundred years ago, he conveyed his frenzied feelings by referring to the canopy vegetation as mere bits of fallen leaves and flowers: "What trees! Coconut trees 50–60 feet high; *Poinciana pulcherrima* with a foot-high bouquet of magnificent bright red flowers; pisang and a host of trees with enormous leaves and scented flowers, as big as the palm of a hand, of which we know nothing. . . . We rush around like the demented; in the first three days we are unable to classify anything; we pick up one object, to throw it away for the next."

To conduct a binocular survey of the canopy, Robin and I in essence enjoyed a leisurely stroll through the forest for a week. During a steady drizzle on day 3, we sat for two hours, getting wet and cold but watching the trees turn into misty shrouds whose canopy treasures were quickly hidden from our wet binoculars. Ground-based work is a fair-weather sport! It was virtually impossible to look up with binoculars during the rain, because droplets collected on the lenses. Seated on a wet log waiting for the rain to stop, I managed to arouse the wrath of many chiggers, whose bites remained with me for several weeks when I returned to the temperate zone.

After suffering the initial pangs of sore neck muscles, we arrived at a routine: walk, check tag number, look up, circle below, look up again, compare observations, ask questions, make morpho-species determinations of new epiphytes, gasp at broken crowns that Robin had never realized were missing, search for the odd missing bole, walk on to the next tree, begin again, and rejoice that each specimen was unique.

Some observations literally leapt out at us. Almost half of the large trees on this well-studied plot had canopies that were in distress — either vine covered, physically damaged by winds or storm, or overtopped by neighbors. Thus, the biological assumption that a large girth at breast height signifies an effective parent tree for recruitment of the next generation is false. Without a healthy crown, a large tree may not be capable of producing a full crop of seeds and ultimately a full crop of foliage with which to continue vigorous growth.

The habit of walking and observing in the woods is perhaps the single most important skill of a field biologist. Our days on Barro Colorado Island resulted in many observations that may stimulate future studies. For example, *Monstera dubia* (family Araceae) was an abundant epiphyte. This aroid had never been really noticed or appreciated by Robin before, but our methodical survey revealed a widespread distribution of both juveniles and adults.

What were the commonest epiphytes on the 50-hectare plot? Much was known about the trees and shrubs of this tract, but next to nothing about its epiphytes. Some epiphytes were relatively rare with a patchy distribution. Others had highly predictable distributions. The orchid *Aspasia* (family Orchidaceae) always grew on main trunks at midcanopy level; *Lomariopsis* (family Lomaripsidaceae) ferns drooped around the buttresses near ground level; many *Maxillaria* and *Pleurothallis* (both family Orchidaceae) grew high up near the crown regions and were too distant to see, other than their silhouettes; and large *Anthurium* (family Araceae) preferred the midtrunk regions just where bright light ceased to filter through.

We were rewarded in our silent walking observations by spider monkeys playing overhead and by a family of tayra (family Mustellidae) perambulating between trees. Wildlife becomes visible when one remains quiet in the forest, and one learns as a human being to appreciate sharing the forest with its denizens.

Despite the fact that over three hundred species of trees grew in close proximity on this plot, it was possible to train our eyes to begin to see patterns. As a botanist, I find it reassuring to recognize a "friendly face" amidst the complex array of green foliage. *Hybanthus prunifolius* (family Violaceae), the most common understory shrub, became easy to spot. In contrast, twenty-one species manifested only one individual throughout the entire 50 hectares. The most common canopy tree, *Trichilia tuberculata* (family Meliaceae), occupied about 12 percent of the canopy (one in every eight trees). Despite its pervasiveness and the fact that many students and scientists have studied aspects of its ecology, the reasons for its success are not known. Alas, it may not be common in the next century!

Throughout the neotropics I frequently observed *Bauhinia* SP. (family Leguminosae), a genus that occupies vine, shrub, and tree habitats. Its unusual hoof-shaped leaves are easy to locate both on the ground and in the canopy. A Peruvian shaman once told me that a special concoction of *Bauhinia* was used to prevent pregnancy in his village, and that another dosage was used for fertility. This plant must have an incredible chemistry! Obviously it is important culturally as well as ecologically in tropical ecosystems.

Walking through the forest with a biologist such as Robin Foster, who has spent many years in this region, was an extraordinary experience. There is so much to observe and to learn in a complex tropical forest. It takes years even to scratch the surface, and Robin has been coming to this site since 1967. He patted special trees and commented on tree falls that had occurred years ago, unusual insect outbreaks, and flowering patterns of different species. One of his favorite individuals was a large *Ceiba pentandra* (family Bombacaceae), a much-photographed tree on BCI with a diameter of more than 20 feet. Robin laughed about the challenge of getting ladders to climb above the flanged buttresses in order to estimate that diameter.

Another fascinating tree was *Tachigalia versicolor* (family Leguminosae), called the suicide tree. This tree was appropriately named,

Bauhinia sp., which grows as a vine, shrub, and tree throughout Central and South America. In Peru a village shaman told me that it is used to promote fertility as well as to discourage it. Obviously, one needs to be careful about the administered dosage! Illustration by Barbara Harrison.

after Robin observed that it flowered and fruited only once as an adult and promptly died. The suicidal behavior appeared to occur in waves, with a cohort of trees undergoing this dramatic event simultaneously. Now when a *Tachigalia* is observed flowering in the plot, scientists can predict its inevitable death and the ensuing creation of a gap in the canopy. Why would a tree evolve such a mechanism for mortality, one wonders? Perhaps this species invests all of its energy into a great burst of reproductive activity, after which it can no longer survive. Robin argued against that, because the tree does not have seeds of disproportionate size compared to other species that do not die after reproduction. The suicide tree does flower for an inordinately long period compared to many other trees and its investment in nectar is high. Obviously, the trade-offs involved in reproduction are not always obvious from our anthropocentric perspective.

Perhaps there are other significant ramifications, such as providing physical space for newly germinated offspring when the parent dies. Observations indicate that the seeds of *Tachigalia* are not dispersed much farther than 100 meters from the adult, so the optimization of space for the next generation is a plausible explanation. However, the seedlings grow very well in the shade and do not seem to require a light gap for successful establishment. Perhaps the gradual erosion of a site in the absence of a parent offers some other advantage to the offspring: gradual changes in soil conditions as the parent tree decays, physical availability of root space, or mycorrhizal associations. (*Mycorrhizae* are fungi that grow in partnership with the roots of some plants and impart a benefit to those plants by taking in more water or nutrients.) These are some of the many ideas about one of the hundreds of tree species in this forest. Clearly, many years are required to unravel the complex patterns of tropical trees.

The 50-hectare plot is only beginning to reap the benefits of the years of work and organization invested in its establishment. Like our long-term project in the Australian forests, the data become more valuable with time. One of the goals of such comprehensive fieldwork is to deduce which forces determine the species dynamics and turnover (or equilibrium) of a tropical forest. The concept of equilibrium could perhaps be explained in terms of whether the trees in a plot have some collective stability, or whether they are in a non-equilibrium state (meaning that the future inhabitants of the site would be less predictable). Hubbell and Foster have found evidence of both equilibrium and nonequilibrium forces in the dynamics of their plot. Species richness can be partially explained by nonequilibrium forces where continual species turnover is possible. Saplings, however, also exhibited higher survivorship away from conspecific trees, suggesting an equilibrium mechanism with density-dependent forces at work. More data are required to examine the equilibrium versus nonequilibrium hypotheses as part of our understanding of tropical-forest dynamics.

Conducting our binocular surveys on BCI prompted a new idea: that we need to compare the accuracy of ground-based observations with what is really up in the canopy. With our walkways we are starting to make this comparison. Using the canopy raft in French Guiana in 1996, Robin and I compared the vine diversity of our ground survey with a (more accurate) canopy exploration. To no one's surprise, we found that our ground-based survey of vines significantly underestimated the diversity and abundance of canopy vines. We plan also to estimate the numbers of epiphytes from ground level, then compare those to accurate counts made in the crown. Only then can we realistically estimate how comprehensive (or how inaccurate) are the ground-based surveys published in the years before canopy access was available as a research tool. Further, we need to establish long-term sites for canopy research. Only after many years of patient data collection can we be certain about many of our observations in the forest canopy. We need to initiate permanent field studies soon, before the further destruction of forests precludes their conservation for future generations.

11 Out on a Limb

A Lady an explorer? A traveller in skirts?
The notion's just a trifle too seraphic;
Let them stay and mind the babies or hem
our ragged shirts;
But they mustn't, can't, and shan't be geographic.
 —*Punch* magazine, June 1893 (reprinted in
Jane Robinson, *Unsuitable for Ladies,* 1996)

When I taught Introduction to Environmental Studies at Williams College, I wanted to assess my students' knowledge of science in order to direct the lectures appropriately. I gave the 110 students a questionnaire on the first day of class. One of the questions (relevant to a tutorial I was planning about women in science) was to name three prominent women scientists. Most students left this question blank or wrote "Don't know any." Several remembered Marie Curie or Rachel Carson, and a few clever students (perhaps future politicians?) listed "Professor Lowman." I offered the tutorial, and went on to organize an entire course on the subject the following year—which, needless to say, fascinated the students.

Why have women been so invisible in science, particularly in field biology and especially in botany?

The developments in canopy research continue fast and furious. Since writing these chapters, I have sailed in a hot-air balloon over French Guiana, witnessed the erection of new canopy cranes in Australia and Panama, worked atop the world's largest canopy walkway in Amazonian Peru, and returned to Peru with Bob Ballard plus a group of students and teachers for Jason X in March 1999. All of these experiences represent more chapters in my life. While working on the canopy walkway in Peru, I measured the first significant herbivory in epiphytes; I also became acquainted with my future husband (not necessarily in that order of priority). My research and my family life have come full circle. The career choices that estranged me from my Australian heritage have led me in new directions that are compatible with both my passion for science and my devotion to family. Nurtured by a sense of discovery, my sons blossom as they grow older and begin to formulate their own perceptions of nature and the world around them.

As I look back on this portion of my life, it is obvious that my science and my personal story were interwoven. Given a magic wand, would I have changed the events that shaped me? Not at all. I might only have wished for a woman mentor or two to provide support and wisdom. Despite the bittersweet taste of some memories, I believe that my times of suffering resulted in important perspective to appreciate the joys of other years. I accept the ups and the downs as a necessary part of becoming a scientist and a person.

I often wonder how I became interested in science, with no family or women mentors to set a precedent. It seems I never questioned the dearth of distinguished women scientists when I was a graduate student. If I had had a female mentor, would I have been better prepared to juggle parenthood and field biology? Could I have minimized my frustrations and setbacks? Yes. I believe that part of my role as a scientist today is to offer friendship and advice, when appropriate, to students who confront challenging issues. In recent years I have developed close friendships with other women in science. All the same, I still admire and seek advice from the original (male) mentors — John Trott, Peter Ashton, Joe Connell, Hal Heatwole — who crystallized my enthusiasm for field biology.

During the thousands of hours that I have spent alone in the forest, nature has imparted wisdom and strength to me, and these gifts are priceless. I still take solace in the example of the fig tree, whose tenacity and unique lifestyle give it a definite advantage in the struggle to attain space in a tropical-forest canopy. Its ability to start at the top and grow down, different in habit from all other trees, has been a valuable lesson for me: taking the road less traveled has its advantages. As a woman in field biology, I find this notion reassuring.

What next? After two decades of climbing trees and going out on many limbs, both literally and figuratively, can I continue to forge new territory in science? The challenges in field biology are enormous. We have only begun to scratch the surface in terms of grappling with biodiversity, and in our ability to synthesize results and

1 foot

Ficus watkinsiana

Figs (*Ficus* sp.), perhaps my favorite trees in the rain forest because of their unique lifestyle. They grow down from the top, thereby guaranteeing a high rate of success in obtaining a canopy position; and they surround and suffocate the host tree, further ensuring a permanent position in the forest canopy. They are important food sources for many birds, insects, and animals. Because of their incredible success, I secretly believe that figs may someday dominate the rain forest. Illustration by Barbara Harrison.

apply them to management and policymaking. Unknown discoveries remain hidden in the forest canopies. Perhaps of utmost priority, our scientific data need to be translated into everyday language for voters, economists, and politicians — individuals who directly affect decisions about the conservation of natural resources. I pray that there will be tracts of natural forest left for my children to enjoy, and I know that the ability of scientists to communicate with the public is vital to forest conservation. After all, the health of our planet depends on insightful policies of forest management.

The last event in the life of a leaf in the treetop is senescence, or leaf fall. In my canopy research, I documented the specific month when each leaf fell from its branch. Further, I measured the rates of decay of leaves on the forest floor. In that sense, my studies of leaves were complete, progressing from beginning to end. In ecology, leaf fall is not the end; it is also the beginning. Through the process of decomposition the contents of a leaf are broken down in the soil and resorbed via root hairs to yield future growth.

Like an aging leaf, my devotion to keeping a nature journal helped me to redigest and reevaluate some of my past. As I reflect on my notes over these two formative decades, I am struck by a rejuvenation of ideas along with a gradual transition into middle age. As I contemplate other professional women, I realize that all of us have stories to share. Maybe the prototype conventional person no longer exists. Many of us have taken circuitous pathways, detouring around obstacles along the way. The difficulties that I encountered as a woman in field biology may, ironically, have strengthened me and led me to stronger convictions. I probably needed this strength to endure the rigors of fieldwork in remote jungles, and to survive the emotional conflicts of going out on a limb in a historically male-dominated culture and profession. Like a leaf with its growth, decay, and rejuvenation, I have experienced a progression in my own personal life and career pathway.

One of the most meaningful insights that I have acquired along my life's journey is that it takes the same amount of energy to complain as it does to exclaim—but the results are incredibly different. Learning to exclaim instead of complain has been my most valuable lesson.

Appendix

Useful equipment handy for a Field Biologist in the
  Rain Forest
comfortable shoes
long pants and long-sleeved shirt (in Australia, I sewed my canvas boots to my pants, to minimize leech invasion)
rain coat
rain hat (especially for those who wear glasses)
handkerchiefs (to wipe one's brow or to remove dirt from one's hand lens)
sunglasses (for driving to and from the field site)
water bottle (to be refilled each night)
small, fold-up umbrella to hold over data sheets
hand lens
Swiss army knife
daypack for supplies
camera and film
compass
tape measure
flashlight (for late returns)
binoculars
notebooks and pencils

field notes and field guides for species identification
waterproof magic markers to label plants
vials to hold insects or other unidentified flying objects
permits (if collecting or working in a restricted area)
maps and checklists for site
first aid kit
insect repellent
toilet paper
plastic bags
energizers (Oreo cookies are my favorite)
tarp (to sit on during lunch and to minimize the dirt, ticks, and
    leeches that tend to lodge in one's private parts)

Glossary

abscission the event when an old leaf breaks at its petiole and falls from the tree

advanced regeneration after germination, a phase (sometimes decades long) when seedlings persist as established individuals on the forest floor, but with very little measurable growth until a light gap occurs overhead

binturong an Asian civet with a prehensile tail

blowfly a persistent fly throughout rural Australia that invades wounds and other vulnerable sites on a sheep to lay its eggs, leading to infection and eventual death of the sheep if not treated

buttress the woody growth at the base of some tropical trees that flares out from the main trunk and appears to offer structural support or to channel rainfall

carabiner an oval metal device used to fasten ropes or secure attachment points for climbing

cassowary a large ostrich-like bird that inhabits the Australian rain forest; only two thousand of this endangered flightless species remain

cauliflory the characteristic of some tropical trees whereby the flowers are borne on the trunk (rather than on branch tips), presumably to facilitate pollination by understory creatures such as bats *cay* a coral island

conspecific in botany, refers to individuals of the same plant species

cool temperate rain forest the wet forest restricted to higher elevation sites in the tropics and extending into the temperate zones; similar to cloud or montane forest

CSIRO Commonwealth Scientific and Industrial Research Organization (in Australia)

cotyledon the first photosynthetic structures on a seedling, which expand when the seed splits open prior to the first pair of leaves

cuscus a marsupial of New Guinea

dirt in construction terminology, the ground-based workers

drip tip a feature of the leaves of tropical trees whereby the point is elongated to a sharp point, presumably to channel water off the leaf during rain showers

ecotone the boundary between two different habitats

epiphylly the covering on leaf surfaces, especially in moist tropical forests; made up of a diversity of organic matter including mosses, lichen, fungi, and microorganisms inhabiting them

epiphyte a plant that lives in the canopies of trees, procuring its nutrients and water from the air and using its host tree only for physical support

flush the event of leafing out synchronously

goanna large monitor lizard

GOLWITS God-of-lone-women-in-tropical-situations; my imaginary savior whenever I found myself in an impossible predicament

Gondawanaland the name for the continents of Australia, Antarctica, and Asia when they were linked together

grazier an Australian rancher, usually the owner of sheep or cattle

gum tree a common Australian term for a eucalypt tree

hammock an ecosystem in which forests exist on slightly elevated patches of land, usually surrounded by wetter ecosystems such as marshes; occurs in Florida *hemiepiphyte* a plant that begins life as an epiphyte and then grows roots into the ground, thereby ceasing to be an epiphyte (e.g., the strangler fig)

herbivory process by which animals consume plants, especially leaves

host specific an organism that is specific to one food plant and will die without it

jumar a mechanical device used for ascent in technical climbing

liana vines

margay a small American wildcat

mast seeder a plant that produces seeds at intervals; an example is the Antarctic beech, which produces seeds only every five years

monodominant a characteristic whereby one species of tree occupies the majority of the canopy

monophagous an organism that feeds exclusively on one food plant

morphospecies differentiation between species but without knowing their true scientific names

mycorrhizae fungi that live in association with the roots of a plant, and may confer an advantage to that individual by enhancing nutrient and water uptake

Oceania the region in the South Pacific that includes Australia, New Zealand, and New Guinea

oropendola a tropical bird that builds a pendulous nest in a communal setting (ten or more birds per tree crown) and has a unique melodious call that is renowned in the tropics

pangolin an Asian and African scaly anteater

patch reefs small reefs separated by expanses of sand

phenology seasonality (e.g., leaf emergence is one phenological event in a canopy)

phylloplane the flat surface of a leaf

pioneer species a colonizing or early settler species on a disturbed or open tract of land, usually succeeded by late successional plant species

property the Australian term for a large ranch or farm

rain forest the forest type typified by complex structure and physiognomy, and more than 2,000 millimeters of rainfall annually

replication part of the careful design of a scientific experiment that involves repeated units or treatments

sclerophyll plants with tough, leathery leaves that resist desiccation and may also be less palatable to herbivores than other plants

sea snake the only snake that inhabits an oceanic environment; one of the most venomous snakes in the world

seed bank the accumulation of seeds that have fallen and lie fallow in the soil, before germination

seed rain the supply of seeds that fall from the canopy to the forest floor

station the Australian term for a large farm, usually containing livestock

subtropical rain forest the forest type that boasts tropical features (such as high diversity of plant forms and species, and buttresses, drip tips, and other traits found in tropical plant families) but is situated in a subtropical latitude

succession the gradual changes in ecosystem composition that occur over time

tropical rain forest the most complex forest type, characterized by high rainfall, homogeneous climate throughout the year, warm and humid weather, a large variety of plant forms, high diversity, and plant species that have tropical origins

viviparous giving birth to live young (e.g., sea snakes)

wallaby a small kangaroo-like herbivore in the Australian bush

warm temperate rain forest the forest type characterized by wet humid environment, situated in the temperate zones at low elevations, and having tree species of both tropical and temperate evolutionary origin

wether a castrated male sheep

whales-tail a metal device for descending on a rope from the treetops

Index

 # A Bird's-Eye Vie

ARCT

ALASKA
(US)

GREENLAND
(DENMARK)

CANADA

UNITED STATES
OF
AMERICA

NORTH

ATLANTIC

OCEAN

1

4

3

2

CENTRAL
AMERICA

12

11

PACIFIC

OCEAN

13

SOUTH
AMERICA

SOUTH

ATLANTIC

OCEAN

14